THE WILD TRIBES OF INDIA

THE
WILD TRIBES
OF
INDIA

HORATIO BICKERSTAFFE ROWNEY

GYAN

Published by

Gyan Publishing House
5, Ansari Road
Daryaganj, New Delhi-110002
Phone: 011-47034999, 9811692060
E-mail: books@gyanbooks.com

Distribution Network
gyanbooks.com
India, USA, Canada, UK, Australia, France

ISBN : 978-81-212-9160-6 (PB)
First Published, 1882

2nd Impression 2023

Printed at: Gyan Press, Delhi.

THE WILD TRIBES OF INDIA
Author: HORATIO BICKERSTAFFE ROWNEY

THE WILD TRIBES OF INDIA.

TRIBES MAP
OF
INDIA
English Miles
AFGHANISTAN
BALUCHISTAN
KASHMEER
CHINESE EMPIRE
THIBET
RAJPUTANA
CENTRAL INDIA
CENTRAL PROVINCES
HYDERABAD
MYSORE
BHUTAN
BURMAH
BRITISH BURMAH
SIAM
ARABIAN SEA
BAY OF BENGAL
ANDAMAN ISLANDS
NICOBAR ISLANDS
LACCADIVE ISLANDS
MALDIVE ISLANDS
CEYLON
Coromandel Coast
Gulf of Siam
Long E. of Greenwich

THE

WILD TRIBES

OF

INDIA

BY

HORATIO BICKERSTAFFE ROWNEY.

Wherein of antres vast and deserts idle,
Rough quarries, rocks, and hills whose heads touch heaven,
It was my hint to speak; . . . . .
And of the Cannibals that each other eat,
The Anthropophagi, and men whose heads
Do grow beneath their shoulders."—OTHELLO.

LONDON:
THOS. DE LA RUE & CO.

1882

CONTENTS.

PART I.

THE INTERNAL TRIBES.

CHAPTER I.

CHAPTER II.

CHAPTER III.

CHAPTER IV.

CHAPTER V.

PART II.

THE FRONTIER TRIBES.

PART III.

THE
WILD TRIBES OF INDIA.

INTRODUCTORY REMARKS.

WITHOUT attaching much importance to the distinctions *Aryan* and *Non-Aryan*, it must be conceded that the population of India may be broadly arranged under two distinct divisions—namely, the *Aboriginal* and the *Immigrant.* Between Kurrachee on one side and Chittagong on the other there are more than a hundred passes through the mountain barriers that invest the country—that is, the Suleiman, the Himalaya, and the Arracan mountains; and these have given various races of invaders admittance into a land famous for its wealth from time anterior to the dawn of legend and chronicle. On the other hand, the sacred books of the country, which are undeniably ancient, are full of the accounts of an indigenous population that existed in it prior to the races of the

Sun and the Moon, and describe minutely the fierce conflicts they waged with the invaders of their hearths and home; and these accounts have evidently a large substratum of truth in them. The aboriginal tribes, we read, were for the most part vanquished and reduced to serfdom, and formed the servile and impurer castes of the Hindu community, amalgamating either wholly or partially with their conquerors. But there were those who did not submit, who fought and receded till they reached parts of the country where the conquerors did not care to seek for them; and there is no reason to doubt that the dark wild tribes of the interior hills and jungles of India, who differ so widely from the inhabitants of the plains, are the remnants of the stubborn *Dasyas* that did not yield. The condition of the conquering race is now well known, for it has been largely written upon; but of the aboriginal tribes who retreated before them the general knowledge is yet very inconsiderable. Every inaccessible jungle, hill-tract, and fen-land of the country is occupied by them; and they are to be seen there even now almost as isolated by manners, language, and prejudices of race from the population by whom they are surrounded as they were in the past. But they are all more or less shy of strangers, and the unhealthiness and inaccessibility of their retreats scarcely invite inquiry or intrusion. We see many parts of the country marked on the maps as "unexplored" or "thinly inhabited," for the best of all reasons that they are malaria-guarded. The English power is of course nominally dominant everywhere; but, in point of fact, these unexplored and thinly inhabited tracts have been to this day only occasionally penetrated here and there by some eager sportsman or zealous missionary, or by an intrepid official whose presence on the spot was required by some exceptional duty. With some of the tribes the outrages perpetrated by them have made our connexion somewhat more intimate than with others; but the information thus collected regarding them is after all but scanty. As a rule the Government officials everywhere have work enough to absorb all their energies, and the jungle and hill tracts receive merely so much of their attention as is absolutely necessary to repel or guard against the raids emanating therefrom. It is scarcely possible under such circumstances to give any very full account of all the wild tribes in the country. What we propose to do is simply to note down within a short compass the little that is actually known at present in regard to their habits, modes of life, and distinguishing peculiarities.

The chief abode of the aboriginal races to be described is the centre of the peninsula—namely, the Vindhya mountains, which run east and west, from the Ganges to Guzerat, and the broad forest-tract extending north and south from the neighbourhood of Allahabad to the banks of the Godavery; but they are not necessarily the aborigines of the places they now occupy. In the *Vedas* the *Dasyas* are spoken of as having given a great deal of trouble and annoyance to the Brahmans; and they were apparently pushed into their present homes by successive tides of invaders operating against them, and often appear as if they were cut off into small parties in their flight, portions of the same race being found scattered in different corners of the country. The main divisions of the *Dasya* race as now seen are: the Gonds, the Bheels, the Kolis, the Mairs and Meenas, the Khonds, the Koles, and the Sonthals; but they are not all one people—at least not at the present day, whatever they may have been in the past. Some particular features they do share in common, such as a common physiognomy, consisting of high cheek-bones, flat noses, and thick lips, a black colour, similar habits of life, and great sameness of character. But the dissimilarities existing between them are also great in several respects, as we shall notice more especially hereafter; and they themselves do not admit any consanguinity with each other. Grouping them according to their obvious affinities, the Gonds are seen congregating in the Central Provinces, the Bheels and Kolis in Western India, the Mairs and Meenás in Rájpootáná, the Koles, Sonthâls, and Dhángurs in Bengal, and the Khonds between Orissá and Madrás; all occupying the wildest parts of each province respectively, all content to be called the "Sons of the Earth" or the "Children of the Forests," while the people of the plains pride themselves on their descent from the Sun and the Moon. The largest number of aborigines are to be seen in the Central Provinces, and the next largest in the Tributary Estates of Bengal; while the most savage specimens are, perhaps, those located within the limits of the Madrás and Bombay Presidencies. There are many smaller communities also scattered all over the peninsula, in every direction except the extreme south, each with a distinct name and with some distinguishing trait peculiar to itself; and on the frontiers—in the west, north, and east—are tribes of half-breeds, or of outsiders who have pierced through and settled, who have for ages passed muster with the aborigines of the country, though still retaining marked traces of their foreign origin—Afghán, Mongolian, or Indo-Burmese—in their features and habits. All these tribes hold themselves distinct and aloof from the people of the plains, though from a desire to rise above their natural condition they are gradually engrafting on their own the most popular beliefs and prejudices of their more civilised neighbours. They are all fit denizens of the places they occupy—namely, the hills and forests of their respective provinces, which, left to themselves, would in a short time be overrun by wild beasts, that multiply in India with such remarkable fecundity. It is the wild tribes alone that keep these in check. Without them there would be no traces of habitation on the hills, no hopes of clearance and settlement in the jungles. It is true that many of these tribes live very much like the wild beasts themselves, but still free—free at least as those wild beasts are. The hatred of tyranny which drove their ancestors to their present retreats survives yet in them, the one redeeming feature in their character being their utter abhorrence of thraldom and despotism.

PART I.

THE INTERNAL TRIBES.

CHAPTER I.

TRIBES OF THE CENTRAL PROVINCES.

THE GONDS.

THE most numerous of the Indian wild tribes are the Gonds, who occupy the Central Provinces (or the very heart of the peninsula), which are divided into two nearly equal halves by the Sátpoorá hills, that run south of the Nermuddá river, east and west. The districts comprised in these Provinces are accordingly grouped into three classes—namely, those lying north of, or above, the hills; those belonging to, or embraced by, the hills; and those lying south of, or below, the hills. The districts of the second division form the hill-region of the entire territory, a great portion of which belonged to Holkár before the Mahrattá wars; but at present the plateau of the hills belongs wholly to the Rájáh of Rewáh, while the valleys in its neighbourhood are owned by the British Government. Some parts of the territory are well suited for European settlement, while the rest are fit only for the habitation of tigers or other wild animals; and it is here that the Gonds have existed for ages, and gradually degenerated. A much larger area was marked out in the older maps of India by the name of *Gondwáná*, or the country of the Gonds, which seems at one time to have included almost all the districts both above and below the Sátpoorá range. The Gonds are understood to have been the earliest settlers throughout this extent—that is, from times as far back as history and tradition reach; while before that period they are supposed to have occupied places further to the north, whence they were driven down by successive tides of immigration from the banks of the Indus. It may at any rate be taken for granted that they are a very ancient people, for they are mentioned by name in the *Purános;* and it is almost equally certain that they were for a long period the ruling nation in the provinces in the wilds of which they now hide themselves.

The first to subjugate the Gonds were the Rájpoots, with whom the upper ten thousand got mixed in course of time, whereby they acquired the name of Ráj Gonds, the traces of whose history can yet be followed. The unmixed Gonds are known to have reigned undisturbed in Gurráh up to A.D. 358, and in Mundlá up to A.D. 634. The throne of the first state was secured by the Rájpoots by marriage, its last Gond Rájáh, Nág Deo, being succeeded by his son-in-law, Jádoo Rái, while Gopál Sháh, the tenth in succession to Jádoo Rái, acquired the throne of Mundlá by conquest, and amalgamated it to that of Gurráh. The four kingdoms finally established by the Ráj Gonds were Mundlá and Gurráh, Deogurh, Kherlá, and Chandá, of which the first dominated over the best part of the Nermuddá Valley, while the second commanded the heart of the Sátpoorá range and the southern slopes and plains up to Nágpore, and the third and fourth the vast wild territory to the south, down to the banks of the Godávery. The dynasties that ruled over these kingdoms were distinct, and they existed up to a short time before the extinction of the Mogul Empire, along with a fifth dynasty that was established later at Wárungul. The Mahomedans had a nominal control over all these States, and we read how the Western Gonds, having rebelled against Akbar, were reduced by him, and how several of the eastern tribes were converted to Mahomedanism by Aurungzebe. But no attempt was ever made by any of the Emperors to wipe out the nationality of the Gonds, or to wrest their possessions from them; and they did not suffer in that way till after the Mahomedan Empire was broken up, while the Mahrattá incursions ebbed and flowed. The severity with which they were treated during this period forced them to retire into the hill and jungle recesses they now occupy, while their country became nominally subject to the Peishwá and other Mahrattá chiefs—to none of whom, however, were they really dependent. They rose up in arms against the English power on Áppa Sáheb of Nágpore seeking refuge with their Rájáh, Chyn Sháh, in the Mahádeo hills; and the history of the campaign of 1818 does speak of some petty reverses sustained there by the British arms. Eventually, the Gonds and the Mahrattás were both subdued, upon which the mountain fastnesses of the former were occupied and dismantled, which was succeeded by many efforts made to cultivate peace and civilisation among them. There are no traces now of the royal Gond families of Mundlá and Kherlá; but the descendants of the princes of Deogurh and Chandá still survive as pensioners of the State.

The Gonds are a remarkable people, and have always kept themselves, in the main at least, quite distinct from all other races. At one time they were known as reckless robbers and cut-throats; but they are generally very inoffensive at present, and extremely shy; and, as a rule, make good cultivators, though some tribes among them are too lazy for any work whatever. In the remote past they seem to have known a more civilised condition, for the *Rig Veda* speaks of the "cities" and "houses" of the *Dasyas*, with whom the Gonds may safely be identified; and remains of Gond architecture of great extent are yet to be met with in the forests of Mundlá, Deogurh,

Kherlá, and Chandá, including traces of roads, embankments, and irrigation-works, which fill the traveller with surprise. Their condition now, however, is very low, though of course exceedingly dissimilar in different places. The political changes they have passed through have divided them into three classes—namely, the *Ássul*, or uncorrupted, Gonds; the Ráj, or Hindu, Gonds; and the Mahomedan Gonds. According to the localities now occupied by them, the best known sub-divisions of the race are the Gurráh Gonds, who inhabit Gurráh, Mundlá, and Bhopál; the Ráj Gonds, who occupy Seonee and Deogurh; the Mánjee Gonds, who inhabit Bustar; the Khullottee Gonds, who occupy the lowlands east and west of the Lánjee hills; the Jarriá Gonds, who occupy Chandá; the Máree Gonds, who live in the wildest parts of the province of Nágpore; and the Koorkee Gonds, who inhabit the Pachmári hills. Besides these, there are Gond colonies eastward, in the Cuttack Tributary Mehals, where they touch the Khonds and the Sours, and westward up to Kándeish and Málwá, where they touch the Bheels. The *Ássul*, or unmixed, Gonds are to be found most largely in the unexplored wildernesses between Chatisgurh and the Godávery, and from the Wyngungá to the eastern Gháts. Their villages are always situated in the midst of the densest jungles, and they live the life of wild men there, and have all the virtues of the wild life in more or less degree, being especially noted for their straightforwardness and honesty, and also for their fearlessness in danger, notwithstanding their extreme shyness of strangers. The Gonds who live in the open country are, on the contrary, remarkable only for their meanness, cowardice, and servility, and have, for the most part, been brought under the control and domination of the Hindu population around them.

The personal peculiarities of the entire race are everywhere nearly the same—namely, a short thick-set frame, flat nose, thick lips, straight hair, and jet-black colour, all of which together give to them a most forbidding appearance. The men shave their heads, leaving only a top-knot, more or less long, which yet further disfigures them ; and the women make themselves hideous by tattooing their faces and thighs. Earrings are worn by both sexes, but by the men on one ear only; the women decking themselves further with a profusion of bead necklaces of every colour and size. At the foot of the mountains, and in the outskirts of the forests, there is some sort of dress and an apology for manners, the females being clad sometimes with leaves, but oftener with a small cotton cloth wound round their loins; while the men pass a yet narrower strip of cloth, the well-known Indian *kopni*, between their thighs, or have at places a short *dhoti* to boast of; but the shades of barbarism become deeper higher up the mountains and in the bosom of the woods, where both men and women—especially among the Mánjee and Máree Gonds—live in a state of nature, with their bodies begrimed with ashes and dirt. Clothing for decency is not understood by these savages, and for warmth they do not mind it, for when the mountain wind is very keen they are content to kindle a roaring fire and sit up around it. If any dressed Gonds appear among them they take alarm and fly, being shy even of their own people when not altogether as barbarous as themselves.

The habits of all the Gonds are uncleanly and degraded, but not equally so in all places. In the gloomier recesses of the forest they live very like the wild beasts around them, subsisting either on roots, berries, and wild honey, eked out by the game they kill with their arrows, or on vermin and reptiles; and these are often to be seen contending with kites and vultures in their eagerness for carrion. Nay, it is said, that in the wilder parts of Chatisgurh, and on the high table-land of Amarkantak, there are tribes yet to be found who cut up and feast on their own relatives and friends when they have become too old or infirm to move about; and it is certain that the Brinjáris, or corn-merchants, who go amongst these people most frequently, never enter the more secluded parts of their country until the gravest protestations of security have been made to them. This, however, is the extreme side of the picture only—not that which is more commonly to be met with. The Gond is excessively indolent and averse to labour, but his hills and forests are very productive, and, where he does labour even a little, he raises with great ease large supplies of the *kootkee* and *kodon*, which grow almost spontaneously, and on which he is content to exist. The process of cultivation followed is that called *dháiyá*, elsewhere known by the name of *jooming*, the only instrument used in it being the hatchet for cutting down trees and brushwood. When the tract to be cultivated has been cleared, the cut jungle is set on fire—that is, as soon as it is dry enough to burn—after which the ashes are distributed on the ground as manure. The seeds to be sown are then strewed over the ashes just before the setting in of the rains; or, when it is a slope that has to be cultivated, they are placed at its upper end, it being left to the rains to wash them down into the ground prepared for them. There is no ploughing or other operation of any kind after this, the crop being left to come up of itself. When it has grown, as it always does in abundance, it is protected with great care against the depredations of the deer and wild hog; and the out-turn thus obtained makes the Gond almost altogether independent of extraneous assistance. In those places where a taste for better kinds of food than the *kootkee* and *kodon* has been acquired, the Gonds depend mainly on the Brinjáris for their supply, receiving from them sugar and salt also, which they have commenced of late to appreciate. The only Gonds who have yet learnt to cultivate by ploughing are those who have had Hindu zemindárs over them, and these are able to raise for themselves various crops of wheat, rice, *jhow*, *urhur*, *channá*, maize, *janerá*, oil-seeds, and tobacco. As a rule the western parts of Gondwáná are more fertile and better watered than the rest, and the progress of civilisation there has accordingly been the greatest. The eastern parts of the country lying nearest to the confines of the Cuttack Tributary Estates have also commenced to improve, and an assimilation with Ooryah manners promises in a short time to convert the tribes there located into nearly the same condition with their neighbours. ×

The tribal divisions among the Gonds are in reality very numerous; but they themselves count twelve-and-a-half tribes only—namely, the Ráj Gonds, Raghuwals, Dadávies, Katulyás, Dholis, Ojhyáls, Thotyáls, Koilábhutuls, Koikopáls, Koláms, Mudyáls, Pádals, and a half-tribe of inferior grade that goes by the same name as the last. The language peculiar to all the septs is the same, and is called *Gondi*, which is spoken throughout their country. There is one tribe called Gours, who, living nearest to the Cuttack frontier, have by some writers been counted along with the Ooryáh tribes. But they are scarcely distinguishable from the Gond races in appearance, disposition, and character, and have blood-relations among them, both to their south and west; besides which it may be noted that the name of "Gour," given to them by the Ooryáhs, is only another way of writing and pronouncing the word *Gond*, which, correctly written, ought to be spelt *Gonṛ*.

The Gonds are the most powerful of all the wild tribes in India, at least in numbers, as they count more than a million-and-a-half persons among them, all muscular in development, as we have described them, but sadly deficient in intelligence. The *Ássul* Gonds, we have said, live in the densest jungles to this day, and almost entirely by themselves; and even the domestic Gonds can hardly be held to congregate. In the depths of the forests the Gond villages seldom count more than five or six huts each, containing in all some fifteen or twenty inhabitants; while very often there is no more than a single hut to be seen within an area of one or two miles, with a sole Gond for its occupant, and a pig or two for his companions. Even in the open country the largest village has never so many as fifty houses, rarely more than thirty or thirty-five, each hut counting from five to eight souls. The buildings are all of the most miserable kind, with walls built of stakes cut from the nearest jungle entwined with rude wicker-work and plastered over with mud, while the roof consists of a thin layer or coating of dried grass, over which are spread some *praus* leaves, and a few battens made of bamboo fastened over all, to prevent the leaves from being blown off by the wind. Inside the conveniences are yet more slender. Of house-furniture there is none at all, beyond some dry gourds kept for bringing water; no bedding to sleep upon, nor platter to eat from, the leaves of the forest serving all such purposes alike. Even the room available to the inmates is exceedingly scanty, so much so that the bachelors of a village have to live apart by themselves, which is a rather common rule among the wild tribes of India generally, and has probably been adopted with a view to keep the sexes apart, though a perfect separation of them is nowhere attempted to be enforced.

Where the seclusion of life is very great, the chief occupation of the Gond still is to rove about his forests, hatchet in hand, almost without any object to secure, but ready at all times to cut down the trees that obstruct his path, or to contend with the wild beasts that go prowling about him. At one time this life was perhaps more congenial to him than now, and more productive also—that is, when he lived by way-laying travellers and plundering them. The country he dwells in is so difficult and pathless as to be full of nooks and corners which no body of troops—Hindu, Mahomedan, or European—has ever been able to penetrate, and there is no unlikelihood therefore in the stories related that the travellers met with in these wilds used frequently to be attacked and killed. In the neighbourhood of Amarkantak especially there was, it is said, a favourite mode of destroying them—namely, by carrying them to the shrines there to offer their devotions, and then cutting them down the moment they had prostrated themselves; and during the earlier years of the British rule in India large numbers of the Gonds were frequently met with going about the open country with no other object than the commission of robberies on a wholesale scale. It has of course become less possible to indulge in such propensities at present, which has contributed not a little to make even the uncorrupted Gonds better behaved and more amenable to authority now than they ever were. But where the opportunity of misbehaving arises the will to be mischievous is never wanting among them; nor are they ever unprepared for such occasions. The arms usually carried by the Gonds are the primitive Hindu weapons, the hatchet, the knife, and the bow and arrows, all of which they wield with equal dexterity. The Mahrattás taught them the use of the matchlock also, when employing them against their enemies; but they have not many of these weapons with them now.

Among the less wild tribes the general occupation at present is breeding swine and buffaloes, and rearing fowls; and it is said of the *Ássul* Gonds that even the fowls reared by them are as wild as themselves. Many Gonds also take employment now as coolies, and have been found able and willing to work at timber-cutting, mining, road-making, and other tasks of similar character. They are assiduous too in collecting fuel, lac, unwrought iron, and whatever else is to be found in their hills and forests. They are not less opposed to labour now than before; but the Brinjáris have succeeded in creating new wants and tastes among them, and the price of the supplies they bring in has to be paid. The *soondi*, or spirit-manufacturer, has also introduced distillery-made spirit into their villages, which likewise has to be purchased; and these two causes together have forced them to be more industrious in utilising the produce of their forests than they were accustomed to be before. It has alienated them at the same time from their sanguinary propensities and habits. Before a relish for salt, sugar, and distillery-made spirit was acquired, the Gond was scarcely approachable; but he cannot do without them now, and that has done more to bring him into order than almost anything else. The influence of the Government has been mainly confined to the suppression of open acts of violence, such as murder and dacoity; the tastes created by the *soondis* and the Brinjáris, and the supplies brought in by them, have contributed yet more towards the establishment of general security all over the country, by rendering the presence of strangers in it a necessity to the savages. This has dissipated their reserve to a great extent, and rendered it possible for the *bunniáh*, the blacksmith, the carpenter, and the weaver to enter their villages in the wake of the Brinjáris and the *soondis*. All the civilisation, in fact, that has penetrated those places has been forced into them by the *soondi*, or the Brinjári, or the zemindár, to which three the Gonds owe more for their improvement than to any Government they have ever lived under. The degradation of their actual condition can indeed hardly be more forcibly described than by the perfectly veracious statement that even the conspicuous presence of the *soondi* amongst them at this moment is not an unmitigated evil. The Government has of course very zealously come forward to remedy this state of things by an offer of that panacea for all misfortunes, the Catechism; but the ignorance of the race is profound, and the schools opened for educating them have nowhere been yet largely availed of.

The religion of the Gonds differs materially among the different classes or tribes we have named; but all the unmixed Gonds worship a common deity, differently called Burrá Deo, Bodá Deo, Báum Deo, or Bodeel Peer, who is generally understood to be a representation of the Sun, to whom human sacrifices used to be offered in the past, the substitute for which now is the image of a man made with straw or other similar materials. Among the other deities venerated are representations of the Moon and Stars; but there are no temples for any of them, all the places of worship being in the open air, and simply enclosed by circular walls of loose stone, while the objects worshipped are represented by some two or three large stones stuck upright and smeared with oil and *sindoor* or vermilion. The name of Bhaváni is also respected, as likewise is the tiger, which is considered to be her *báhun*, or riding-animal. The Gonds thread the jungle-paths at dead of night without the slightest dread of the tiger; but they seldom attack it except when it commits great havoc among their cattle. The belief in supernatural agents, too, is widespread amongst them, and so is the fear of witchcraft and of the evil eye; and there is nothing they will not do to guard themselves against these influences.

Of the more remarkable customs among them those relating to marriage and death have some peculiarities in them that may here be cursorily referred to. As said before, the separation of the sexes is provided for by them, but is never very rigidly enforced. The youths of both sexes, though they are not allowed to sleep under the same roof at night, have every facility given to them to meet with and make love to each other at all hours, though the final marriage-arrangements always require the sanction of their parents. The process followed after this sanction has been secured is for the bridegroom to go forth with his friends to fetch his bride home, when she affects to be averse to the union, or not to like a married life at all, and hides herself. This leads to her being sought for, and, on being found, which she always manages should be the case, she is borne off in triumph, after which a great feast is given by the bridegroom's father to celebrate the event, a cow being killed, and a large supply of *lundi* (the favourite drink of the race), provided for. The cow is eaten by all the *Ássul* and the Mahomedan Gonds, but not by the Ráj Gonds, though it is doubtful if the latter stop short of any animal besides the cow. Over the dead, also, the wild Gonds hold a "wake," all the friends of the deceased being summoned to a mourning-feast, which is in every respect very similar to that given on marriage occasions, and, like it, terminates invariably in excess. As a rule the dead are buried, cremation being performed in especial cases only, when the ashes are interred on the roadside.

The diet of the Gonds is, we have stated, comparatively poor, and excessively filthy; and they have had at all times an inveterate taste for drink, which the introduction of the distillery system in their country has yet further aggravated. They are also great smokers, and he that has no clothing on his body has still a girdle of *cowries* or cords around his waist to suspend therefrom a tobacco-pouch alongside of a naked knife. And yet, notwithstanding such deleterious habits, they are found in all places to be long-lived, and do not soon exhibit signs of old age, retaining sound teeth and black hair almost to the day of their death. Improved food and improved clothing, improved habitations and improved hygiene, are of course as desirable for them as for every other race similarly circumstanced; but they have thriven so well without them hitherto, that the more pressing requirements in their case seem rather to be the introduction of better habits of usefulness and a better appreciation of sustained labour by finding suitable work for them in the midst of their own wildernesses, which they will not abandon for the very best advantages. They are very deficient in intelligence also, but, as they are tractable and obedient under kind treatment, there ought to be no insuperable impediment in the way of improving them even in this respect. They are among the best behaved of the wild tribes now, whatever they may have been before, and on that account, if for nothing else, deserve that everything that can be done for them should be done.

MINOR TRIBES OF THE CENTRAL PROVINCES.

The wild tribes in the Central Provinces include a sprinkling of Kolis and Bheels; but, as these are more powerfully located elsewhere, we shall not allude to them in this place. There are also a great many minor tribes in the country—too many in fact for all of them to be even named by us; but out of them the Brinjáris, already referred to, the Bhowris, or Hareen Shikáris, the Táreemooks, or wandering blacksmiths, the Koráwars, the Bhátoos, and the Mudikpors, may be enumerated.

THE BRINJÁRIS.

The Brinjáris are wandering traders, who derive their name from their occupation, and are of various tribes. They were called into existence by the necessities of the Hindu and Mahomedan sovereigns, who wanted expert purveyors for their armies, having never had any commissariat department attached to them; and no great body of men could move about the country formerly without being accompanied by these itinerant grainsellers, who were well protected by all. Their original occupation is now gone; but they still go about as before, always in large troops, and accompanied by their families, dogs, and laden bullocks, passing from village to village to supply the wants of the inhabitants, who are all more or less dependent on these visits, even for the very necessaries of life. They are molested by none, though there is hardly any part of India which they do not go to; but in some places they are compelled to pay some trifling duties for the protection extended to them. It is scarcely correct to say that they belong to the Central Provinces in particular, or to any other part of India, for they come and go from place to place without forming any permanent attachments anywhere. They are most frequently seen in Central India, because their services are in particular demand there, on account of the indolence of the Gonds, whom they supply with food-grains purchased from the zemindárs, and more especially with salt, sugar, and other luxuries, receiving in exchange the productions of their wilds, which they carry to more profitable markets. They pursue their course through roads which nothing but the most indefatigable spirit of industry could induce anyone to attempt, and through narrow defiles often barely affording passage to them and their bullocks. The men are tall and well formed, dressing very like the communities among whom they move, and having similar manners to a great extent. Born in the open field, and bred up as itinerants, they brave the heat of a vertical sun, the bleak blasts of winter, and the deluges of the rainy season with equal indifference, and in so doing acquire a robust constitution which is shared by their women. They live mostly under tents, except during the rains, when they set up temporary grass-huts wherever they may be stopping at the time. Though nearly as rude as most of the tribes they mix with, they acquire by necessity some acquaintance with the arts of life, and are also more industrious than all of them; but they are poorer now than they were before, and with their poverty have become more criminal too—robbers, cattle-lifters, and Thugs having been found among them.

THE BHOWRIS.

The Bhowris are also a vagabond race, of shorter stature than the Brinjáris, and unlike them in this, too, that they are very shy and unintelligent, almost equally so with the Gonds. They, too, are to be seen in all parts of India, like the Brinjáris, and figure similarly as thieves on a large scale, though gang-robbery and offences attended with violence are out of their line. They hunt wild animals of all kinds, and eat whatever they kill. Their manners are very rude; they have hardly any dress at all—nothing in fact beyond a narrow loin-cloth; and the women are no better clad than the men. They are nevertheless very thrifty; and professional dacoits are always on the look-out for them.

THE TÁREEMOOKS.

The Táreemooks, on the contrary, are a poor and improvident race, living from hand to mouth. They are of a dark colour, though not quite so dark as the Gonds and some of the other tribes, and are a little taller and better formed than all of them. They are very laborious also, and are always loyally assisted in their labours by their women, who collect wood in the jungles to make charcoal for them, and work their forge-bellows; but they cannot, for all that, make the two ends meet, principally from being much addicted to drink. The life of the tribe, moreover, is very loose; there is no such thing as constancy among the men or chastity among the women; and married men make love to each other's wives almost openly, without fear or shame.

THE KORÁWARS.

The Koráwars are of shorter stature, but are otherwise as robustly made as the Táreemooks, having well-knit muscular frames and a large share of energy. They are divided into many sects, some of whom are nomadic and constantly roving, while others lead a settled life. They cultivate a little for themselves, and also make grass-screens and baskets ; but they always have more money than can ever be earned by such occupations, and the inference is that they live mainly as dacoits. Their private morals too are very low, and many among them make money by prostituting their women, who are trained up as dancing girls, and attached to the temples as *debnuttees*, or mistresses of the gods. These women bear children, but that entails no disgrace either on them or on their progeny.

THE BHÁTOOS.

The Bhátoos are a short-sized but well-formed and active race, trained to agile feats from their youth. The exhibition of these feats is their ostensible means of living, and they wander from village to village displaying their nimbleness with the aid of a bamboo, which is worshipped as a god. They call themselves Mahrattás, but the genuine Mahrattás do not acknowledge any relationship with them.

THE MUDIKPORS.

The Mudikpors are tall powerful men, having olive-yellow complexions, and are fishermen by trade, while their women earn a little by knitting and tattooing. They bear the best character of all the minor tribes named, and their females are especially spoken of as being equally honest and assiduous.

CHAPTER II.

TRIBES IN WESTERN INDIA.

THE BHEELS.

THE Bheels are numerically inferior to the Gonds, but are in all other respects a more important race. Their country is called *Bheelwárá*, and embraces the rocky ranges of the Vindhyá, Sátpoorá, and Sátmálli mountains, of which the passes were long held by them; and the jungles on both banks of the Nermuddá, the Táptee, and the Máhee. Popular tradition ascribes to them a fabulous origin from Mahádeva, who is said to have fallen in love with a forest girl, by whom he had a numerous progeny, one of the children being particularly ugly and vicious, who distinguished himself finally by slaying his father's favourite *brisa*, or bull, for which he was expelled from the habitations of men. The Bheels pretend to be descended from this outcast, and to have inherited crime and outlawry as "Mahádeva's thieves"—that is, with their descent. They are divided into so many tribes that the opinion has been hazarded that the name "Bheel," when it was originally assumed, perhaps only denoted a confederacy of various robber-races thrown together and associated by local circumstances and events; but the inference is far-fetched and scarcely tenable, for the Bheels are mentioned as an aboriginal people in the *Mahábhárata*, and the history of India shows that, like the Gonds, they were at one time a ruling race, though not exactly in the places they now occupy. Their original residence, it is supposed, was Márwár or Jodhpore, whence they were driven south by other races; and the local history of the Rájpoot princes confirms the belief by stating that the Bheels were expelled from the plain country by the Rájpoots. Their present quarters were apparently sought for by them in preference to subjection and civilisation when the tides of immigration and conquest were running too strong to be breasted, and, becoming masters of the mountain-passes to which they had retreated, they felt that they were unconquerable, and retained for good the positions they had occupied. The hill tracts of Kándeish and Málwá have thus belonged to them from very remote times; and, as none of the native Governments were ever powerful enough to restrain their lawlessness effectually, their depredations on the rich lowlanders in their immediate vicinity were early commenced and persistently continued. They regarded it, in fact, as their privilege to rob, and, besides always oppressing their neighbours, took advantage of every change in the administration and every internal commotion to sally forth to greater distances in quest of victims. Their demands for black mail were openly made, and many of them were conveyed in writing, the scraps being left dangling round the neck of some village idol, or from some well-known tree, before the village was attacked. One of these notes has been thus translated :—

"From Mohun Náik
"To Bholá, Pátel of Keeprá Kairá,

"The moment you receive this note you must bring Rs. 500, which are due to us. If any delay occurs we will put your people to death, cut off their ears and noses, and help ourselves. Let this be well considered."

And the threats thus held out were invariably carried into effect. All that the administrators of the country were able to do in return was to entice the robbers into their power by deceit and stratagem, and those who fell into the snare were generally very summarily dealt with. During the period of Mahrattá rule especially the Bheels were entrapped in large numbers under hopes of pardon and preferment, and then massacred without remorse. They were viewed simply as pests and outcasts of society, to exterminate whom any artifice was held to be justifiable; but nothing that could be done in that way was ever able to check their depredations, and their turbulence had full play down to the falling off of the Mahomedan power. In fact, at this period the Bheels seem to have advanced more than ever in political strength and status, the struggles between the Mahomedans and the Mahrattás, and the subsequent misgovernment of the Peishwá's officers, having given them the opportunity to start organised bands of dacoits in every direction, headed by Náiks, or chiefs, who assumed all the state of petty princes, and desolated every village or hamlet that was accessible to them. This state of disorder was prolonged till the establishment of the English rule in India, when, the plundering habits of the Bheels bringing them into conflict with that power, Kándeish and Málwá were occupied by Sir John Malcolm in 1818, during the great Mahrattá and Pindári war, whereby the political authority of the caterans was terminated.

The first measures taken by the British Government to subdue the Bheels were to stop the supplies of food drawn by them from the plains, and simultaneously to cut off all parties attempting to issue from the hills for purposes of plunder. These steps proving unsuccessful, recourse was had to military operations; and in the struggles that followed many chiefs were killed, while those who were captured were imprisoned, or transported, or hanged. The power of the British arms was now felt to be irresistible; but the Bheels did not yet betray any wish to give in, and fresh chiefs started up to replace those who had been taken and punished. This forced on the Government the adoption of milder measures, which were commenced by the offer of a general amnesty to all who would submit, with the exception of the most heinous offenders. "You have lived in the hills and plundered the roads and the country," said the proclamation that was issued; "the *Sirkár* has pardoned your past crimes, and you may remain in your villages if you will cultivate the lands and gain your livelihood honestly." With a free pardon were also offered lands, clothes, money, and food; and that many still held out was owing only to their dread of such deceit as had been frequently practised on them before by the native Governments, which always destroyed those whom they were able to entrap. When they found, however, that their fears were groundless, they began to come in in large numbers, and to settle down quietly in different places as *pátels*, or cultivators of the soil; upon which they were furnished with food and the implements of husbandry to learn the new life that was opened out to them, while the possession of their lands was secured to them, with freedom from taxation for a number of years, to make it worth their while to acquire industrious habits. This led to the establishment of the Bheel Agency in 1825, to watch over the colonies that were formed, military operations being thenceforth confined to the pursuit of the armed bands that still infested the wilder parts of the country, which gave almost as much trouble as they experienced themselves, the utmost efforts of the harnessed soldier being often quite powerless to cope with them on equal terms. The last reformatory measure adopted, therefore, was the organisation of a military corps, which all the unruly Bheels were invited to enter, and which necessarily contributed most of all to the eventual pacification of the country. All classes of Bheels now began to submit in large numbers, though not without occasional protests against restraint and subjection to law; and the habits of the entire nation were thus gradually changed. The corps did particular service in putting down the plundering proclivities of their countrymen, whereby the reforms introduced by the Agency were allowed time to operate on their character, and to refashion it. One officer, in writing of the people in 1855, says that, "Instead of living chiefly on plunder, as we found them doing, it is seldom that any of them are guilty even of petty gang robbery." This was an official picture, and over-coloured to a considerable extent; but within the last sixty years the bulk of a people who were found utterly savage to commence with have, at least apparently, become reconciled to the peaceful and industrious life that was chalked out for them. In Kándeish the Bheels form about one-eighth of the population, and are among the best behaved and most useful. A great many of them are wholly devoted to agriculture, and, though it cannot be said that they have become very successful and prosperous farmers, still in most places they have become apt to this extent, that they are not easily distinguishable from the other cultivating classes around them. Many of them, also, make their living by the manufacture of baskets, in which they are very skilful; others collect gums, wax, and honey, and barter them for the produce of the surrounding countries; others cut and sell firewood and timber, and all the fruits, roots, and herbs of the jungles; others take service as ploughmen and day-labourers on the plains; others kill wild animals for the sake of the rewards given for them; while others are serving as soldiers in the Bheel corps, which is distributed over the province in numerous detachments, and mainly employed on police duties. Similarly, the Bheels of Guzerát, who are settled about the banks of the Máhee, are now engaged almost exclusively in agriculture; while those of Indore, in Holkár's dominions, who were at one time among the most wild and savage, have been largely converted into useful and trustworthy soldiers, and are fast acquiring agricultural habits also.

The physical characteristics of the Bheels are: a dark colour, diminutive size, prominent cheek-bones, large nostrils, and great personal activity combined with an astonishing power of enduring fatigue. They are not so long-lived as the Gonds, and become old at sixty, at which age a Gond usually shows no signs of decay; but they have more hardihood and agility than the Gonds, though less of muscular strength and are so restless by disposition that nothing is able to reconcile them to purely sedentary pursuits. The main divisions of the race are known as the village, the cultivating, and the wild or mountain Bheels; of whom the first comprise all those who, from chance or ancient residence, have become inhabitants of the villages of the plains in the immediate neighbourhood of the hills; the second, all those who have continued in their peaceable occupations ever since their gangs were broken up and their leaders destroyed or driven abroad; and the third, those who, preferring savage freedom to a life of comparative comfort under control, live almost as wild now as before, in the wildest parts of their mountain country. Of these classes the second and the third have alternately increased or decreased in numbers according to the fluctuations of the neighbouring Governments, and are essentially the same to this day in almost every respect. When the Governments were strong, the cultivating Bheels always drew recruits from the ranks of their wilder brethren; while, when the Governments were weak or oppressive, the industrious Bheels were driven by their behaviour to join the robber-tribes and adopt their profession for the time. The village Bheels, on the contrary, have for a long period lived quite apart from both the other classes, holding as little intercourse with them as men of the same race, living in the same manner generally, and almost side by side with each other, could possibly manage. Distinguished locally, the chief tribes now residing within British territory are: the Naháls, the Nirdhis, the Khoteels, and the Dáungchees, who still live apart from all others in their mountains and jungles; and the Turvees, the Mutwárees, the Burdás, the Dorepies, the Mowchees, the Parvees, the Wulvees, the Wusáwás, the Wurálás, and the Powerás, most of whom have long subsided into peaceful inhabitants under the fostering care of a benevolent Government. The Naháls inhabit the north-east part of Kándeish, from Arráwád to Boorhánpore, and have a name for untameableness to this day, together with all the wild habits with which their ancestors were credited, living on wild fruits and roots mainly, and on the game obtained by their archery. The character of the Nirdhis, who live about the Ajuntá range, is very similar, and includes a thorough contempt and dislike of labour as it is understood by the more civilised tribes. The Khoteels are the wild inhabitants of the Sátpoorá hills, who, however, collect gums and wax with great patience, and barter them for the produce of the plains. The Dáungchees are the natives of the Dáung below the Western Ghats, and have the reputation of being the most degraded, the most stupid, and the most uncivilised of all the tribes. Of the other clans the Turvees are the neighbours of the Naháls, and live between Arráwád and Boorhánpore, where they are best known at present for their devotion to agriculture, though they bore a more disorderly character during the Pindári times; the Mutwárees, Burdás, and Dorepies inhabit the mountain ranges to the north-west of Kándeish about Akránee and Dhergong, and are famed for their skill in basket-making, besides being good cultivators also; while the Mowchees, Parvees, Wulvees, Wusáwás, Wurálás, and Powerás, who inhabit the western districts of Sultánpore, Tikree, etc., are particularly distinguished for their pastoral habits, and some of them, such as the Wurálás, also for rearing domestic fowls in great abundance. There are some Bheel tribes besides in Áhmedábád and Rewáh Kantá, who are named Bariá, Karit, Pággi, Kotwál, and Naikrá; and many among these are adepts in cattle-lifting and thieving, though they have yet more generally betaken to agriculture at the present day.

All the Bheel tribes do not resemble each other; for, while the Dáungchees, for instance, are of the darkest colour and have a forbidding appearance, the Turvees have a fairer skin and finer features, the difference between them in other respects being equally remarkable. But the reason for this is not far to find. The Mogul policy located Mahomedan colonists among the Bheels, in the hope of keeping them in check, and perhaps of civilising them. But the colonists fraternised with the people they were appointed to watch over, and got mixed with them, the only service they did to their Government being confined to the conversion of many Bheel tribes to Mahomedanism. The Turvees are believed to be the descendants of these colonists, while the Dáung-chees represent the unadulterated race; both equally illiterate, but one quick and intelligent, the other having intellect barely enough to understand the simplest communications, and totally unequal to comprehend anything beyond them. In some cases the differences between the tribes are so great that it is often impossible to find any common ground of affinity between them. But this upon inquiry is invariably found to be the sequence of gradual reclamation only.

The country of the Bheels is still as wild as ever; but a great portion of the population, we have seen, has now been thoroughly tamed, and accustomed to industry and labour. The tribes are distinct in some respects, which we have partially noticed, and, while some are Hindus, others are Mahomedans, a few again being neither one nor the other. Even the languages spoken by them severally are not the same, at least in all places. But still are they one people, living almost on the same diet, having the same usages generally, and bearing the same character slightly diversified under the distinctions of "wild" and "reformed," by which they are mainly distinguished. The particulars to be noticed of them are necessarily in a great measure identical. They are all wholly illiterate, and some so ignorant that they cannot count, and have no terms to express numbers beyond twenty; and the schools which have been opened for them by the Government have nowhere been much availed of. But they have expression in their eyes and features, and, though unable to read and write, have an intelligence which develops with their condition. In the mountains the wild Bheels still remain in a state of nature; but the bulk of those who inhabit the valleys have always a belt of coarse cloth round their loins, in which they also carry their knives, and some wrap a second piece of cloth besides round their heads and shoulders. The women are even more decently clad than the men, and are less dirty than the women of the Gonds; and it is said that they are permitted to assert their rights pretty freely over their husbands. The beard and hair of the men used to be kept thick and dishevelled before, which gave them a wild appearance, and this was very much heightened when they went armed; but at present the men shave their faces, and seldom exhibit anything more than a slight moustache, and, far from being dreaded, they are themselves getting distrustful and timid. The arms of the Bheels are the same with those of the Gonds—namely, the axe, the knife, and the bow and arrows, the latter two made of the bamboo, the arrows being tipped with iron heads; and they are all excellent woodmen and ready hunters to this day. They are good workmen also, if their patience be not too severely taxed, and they build their own huts and make their own roads and fences. The huts are made of bamboos, wattled with long grass, and thatched with the same material, with boughs laid over them to guard them against the wind. The buildings are extremely rude, but still more artistic than those of the Gonds; and every house has always a separate thatched enclosure for sheltering cattle, while the fields are surrounded with high fences of boughs and bamboos, to keep out the deer and antelopes from the corn. Having been thieves and robbers for centuries, the men are still very careful in protecting their villages, and the approach of a stranger is always announced by a shrill scream, which puts every one on his guard; and, unlike the Gond fashion, their huts are always crowded close together, as if for mutual protection. But they are not inhospitable, and, merry of heart and unused to the bonds of society, receive every wayfarer with a gaiety peculiar to them, and are always assiduous in making him comfortable. The chief defects still observable in their character are that, though restless and active, they are very impatient, and will stick to no continuous work if they can do without it. They are full of life and spirits, and will rove or hunt through their forests all day, or commit the most daring robberies in those parts of the country where such things can yet be perpetrated with impunity; but still they will rather live on half rations in idleness than on a full diet with labour. They are also excessively fond of liquor and tobacco, their favourite beverage being a spirit distilled from the *mohowá* flower, which is freely supplied to them by the enterprising Pársee, who has shops for vending it even in the wilderness, and sells it for grain, grass, wood, or anything that his customers will pay. The tobacco is smoked rolled up in the form of a cigar inside the leaf of the *áptá* tree, and the smoking is almost continuous. They are, moreover, very filthy eaters, like the Gonds, and, though their staple food is maize and rice, they reject nothing, devouring meat of all kinds with eagerness, including that of foxes, jackals, and snakes, and often when in a putrid state. Many of them have become farmers, but are hardly even now well reconciled to the change; some are hunters by necessity; others live almost entirely on the produce of their forests: what they are all equally apt for yet is leading the same wild life that originally belonged to them, notwithstanding the timidity the plain Bheels seemingly evince. Much has been already done to civilise them, and the amelioration system is still being worked out; but it almost seems that if they were left to themselves for a few years it would not cost them much to relapse to their old habits and ways. When trusted they are the trustiest of men, and as a rule they are preferred to other wild tribes generally for service in the police and in gentlemen's houses; but the occasional excesses they even now commit indicate clearly what they would be again if they could have their own way as before.

Among the redeeming features of the Bheel character are: great attachment for home and family, kindness towards women, respect for their elders, and an unsophisticated love for truth. A Bheel will never tell a lie; and he is generally so simple-hearted that, on being apprehended as an offender, he will not only confess all his transgressions, past and present, but will betray all his accomplices. As regards the position of the Bheel elders, the oldest man in each village is still always looked up to as its chief, and vested with a sort of patriarchal authority over the other villagers, which he exercises, however, by sufferance only, not by right; and, similarly, the domestic virtues are generally well cultivated, but without the ties being strongly and lawfully bound. The selection of a wife is always made by every Bheel himself, after which he enters into a formal engagement with the girl chosen at the foot of the *singá* tree, which is held to be particularly sacred; but there are no ceremonies of any kind to give validity to the engagement. When the marriage-day is fixed, the female relatives of the bridegroom force themselves into the house of the bride, and carry her off *vi et armis;* and, on her being brought to her lover, the marriage ceremony is completed, usually with a feast. But the parties thus united are not irrevocably bound. Generally they love each other, and the Bheel husband has always had the credit of allowing his wife to domineer over him. But they live in concert so long only as they choose, and separate at pleasure or convenience, the grown-up children being left with the father, while the younger ones are carried away by the mother. Polygamy is also practised, which necessarily qualifies the love of the husband for his wife; and, where there are several wives, the family house is seldom an abode of peace. As to religion, the ideas of the Bheels are based mainly on Hinduism, though not conforming to it very loyally. The chief deities recognised by the mountain tribes are named Sudál Deo, Kumbáh Deo, and Mámniá Dánip; the first of whom is worshipped in conjunction with the Sun and the Moon, and is supposed to have the elements under his control; the second, at the *Dewáli*, acting apparently as a substitute for the goddess Káli; while the third is the Ceres of the mountains—the dispenser of the bounties of the earth, at whose shrine the first fruits of the season are offered. We read, also, that the Ághori worship of Devi, in her most terrific forms, was at one time constantly celebrated by the mountaineers, and was always accompanied by human sacrifices, the *Vrihat Kathá* being full of stories on the subject, all the scenes describing which are laid in the Vindhyá range. Like the Gonds, however, the Bheels have no temples to worship their gods in, the usual place of worship being the foot of a large tree, where the objects of adoration are represented by big stones placed on a platform of mud. Adoration is also offered by them to their ancestors, the tiger, and the infernal spirits, the last of whom especially are very much feared; and sacrifices are likewise made to several of the minor Hindu deities to propitiate their favour. Witchcraft and omens, too, are believed in, as they are by almost all the wild tribes; and the *Holi* and the *Dasahárá* are celebrated as affording opportunities for a debauch. There is usually a debauch also over the dead, of whom the males are burnt along with their arms and cooking utensils; while the females and children are buried, and a cairn of stones heaped over each grave.

THE KOLIS.

The Bheels extend westward to Guzerát, where they meet the Kolis, just as they extend eastward to Gondwáná, where they touch the Gonds. The especial seat of the Kolis is the country north of the river Máhee, the bulk of the population along the entire north-west frontier of Guzerát being also formed of them. They are a robust and bold-looking people, having the same physical peculiarities as the Bheels, and were long equally well known as enterprising thieves and plunderers, possessed of many hill-forts, which were all dismantled after the great Mahrattá war. The Bheels regard them as being of the same family with themselves; but the Kolis do not acknowledge the relationship. Living side by side with each other, the character and habits of the two races are naturally identical to a considerable extent; but the Kolis, having become Hinduised to a greater degree, consider themselves to be of higher caste, and, though they do not object to marry Bheel women, will not allow their own women to marry with the Bheels. There is otherwise so little difference between them that Bishop Heber thought that the Kolis were only civilised Bheels, who had laid aside some of the wilder habits of their ancestors, and sobered down to their present state. But this inference can hardly be justified, for the Kolis have been generally recognised as the original inhabitants of Guzerát, which the Bheels were not; and, as regards wildness of character, the former have always shown themselves to be a shade bloodier and more untameable even than the latter. Of both races the wilder tribes are still predatory where they can manage to be so with impunity; and they are certainly equally averse to honest labour and industry. Though claiming to be Hindus, the Kolis eat animals and vermin of all kinds, like the Bheels, excepting the cow and the village hog; nor object to do so when they have died a natural death. They are also inveterate drunkards, and addicted to the use of opium and *bháng;* and, in short, have all the habits which distinguish the most degraded specimens of the human race, despising every approach to civilisation and decency as indicative of cowardice. When the whole of Guzerát was occupied by them, it was extremely difficult for merchants and pilgrims to pass through their country; and their raids on fairs and religious gatherings are said to have been incessant. They were also largely employed by the native chiefs in desolating each other's territories, and had the reputation of being the most formidable perpetrators of gang-robbery. The arms borne by them were the knife, and the bow and arrows, to which swords and matchlocks were added by those who employed them. At present the chief theatre of their activity is the sea-coast, as far down almost as Goá, where, until lately, they were employed in fishing and piracy; but elsewhere they are seen living peaceably, as part of the general population around them. The chief tribes living near the sea are: the Ráj Kolis, who are cultivators and labourers; the Solesy Kolis, who are also agriculturists; the Towkry Kolis, who cut bamboos for sale, and derive their name from their occupation; the Dhour Kolis, who live principally as labourers, but are better known for their degraded habits; the Doongury Kolis, who are similarly employed and characterised; the Mullár Kolis, who form the most respectable of all the septs, and subsist chiefly by supplying villagers and way-farers with water and other conveniences; the Áheer Kolis, who are herdsmen, as the name implies; the

Murvee Kolis, who are very like the Murvee Bheels, and live mainly as palankeen bearers and porters; and the Sone Kolis, who are fishermen and pirates. The chief tribes in Guzerát are called: the Tullubdáh, Pultunwárriá, Kákrez, Dháundhám, and Bábriáh Kolis, of whom the first are the most numerous, and superior to the others in rank. They are all agriculturists, and grow wheat, *dál*, maize, sugar-cane, and vegetables in large quantities, and rice also, of which the finer kinds are sold to the grain-merchants, while the coarser kinds are consumed by themselves. Their women work with them in the fields, and, though naturally well formed, are so hard worked as soon to lose all traces of their comeliness. The religion professed by them is Hinduism, all the gods of which are venerated and worshipped; and the charms and amulets worn by the Hindus are also in common use among them.

THE GRÁSSIÁS

The Grássiás are another wild people belonging to Guzerát, and are also found in Málwá, in both of which places they were at one time noted for their robberies. They have no claim to the distinction of tribe or caste, being the refuse of all tribes, and derive their name from the free lands which were held by their ancestors. The Bheels and other jungle robbers having greatly disturbed the country by their incursions, the Nawábs of Surát, in the reign of Ferokesere, submitted to a compromise with them, and ceded certain lands in each village which were denominated *todá gyráus*, or exempt from taxation. The holders of these estates enlisted banditti of every caste and country around them, and the descendants of these robbers are the Grássiás. The main divisions among them now are: the Rájpoot and Mahomedan Grássiás respectively—the former sub-divided into two tribes, named the Jhárejás and the Wagelás, and the latter into ten or twelve tribes. The Rájpoot tribes are, both of them, very ignorant and indolent, and destitute alike of spirit and honour, and even of jealousy for their feudal rights and privileges, their whole time being taken up with sensual pleasures and the most injurious abuse of intoxicating drugs and liquors. Of the Mahomedan Grássiás there is nothing particular to notice.

The Káttis.

A more prominent tribe in Western India are the Káttis, who form the majority of the inhabitants of Káttywár. Their name is derived from the word *kát*, or wood, from which they affect to have been produced. The story runs that a man sprang from the rod of Karna—the half-brother and adversary of the Pándavas—on its being split up, and that the task of carrying off the cattle belonging to those warriors from Berut, where they were living in privacy, was assigned to him. Kát was assured by Karna that the gods would never reckon robbery, and especially cattle-lifting, as a sin in him and his descendants, and the Káttis thus claim a divine ordinance and privilege to steal. Some writers affect that they are the same as the Cathaei who opposed the progress of Alexander in the Punjáb. They are certainly a large, well-formed race, athletic and bony, with expressive but harsh features, fair hair and complexion, and light-blue eyes, totally dissimilar in their appearance to the Kolis and the Bheels. Their women are proverbially beautiful, though almost masculine in size and make, while those of the Bheels, if not of the Kolis also, are ugly; and the legend is right in giving them a foreign descent from the earlier Scythians, which Karna and the Pándavas were. But they are outlaws all the same, and attach no disgrace or reproach to the mode of life they have always followed. Originally, they seem to have been of pastoral habits, and lived on the great wastes of Western India in hordes with their flocks; but even then their chief occupations were rapine and plunder. They had chiefs of their own to lead them, and gave asylum to outlaws of every description, whom they employed as mercenaries, not being a numerous tribe themselves. They paid these associates liberally, but never allowed them a share in the robbery, the profit and loss of every adventure being always their own; and they acquired large possessions in this way during the general anarchy produced by the decline of the Mahomedan power. It is scarcely thre hundred years since they have settled in villages and betaken to fixed pursuits. As seen at present, almost every Kátti village has from two to four hundred goats, and sheep, cows, and buffaloes in proportion. The people were averse to cultivation before, but have betaken to that also gradually. But the occupation most pleasant to all of them is the breeding of horses—and they were at one time particularly formidable from the excellence of the horses they bred, when, well mounted and lance in hand, they collected black-mail alike from friend and foe. These horses were never shod, but yet travelled at great speed over the most stony countries without laming. No native robber, in fact, ever considers himself safe over a shod horse, for, if a shoe falls off, he is sure to be taken, since no horse accustomed to shoes can travel without them.

At this moment the Káttis are shepherds, cultivators, and thieves, by turns or together, as suits them best, and not less inclined to brigandage than before, if not strictly looked after; but they are more civilised than the Bheels and Kolis, large-hearted and hospitable, and keenly alive to their honour. Though treacherous to each other, they will never betray their guests. Their dress is decent, very much like that of the Rájpoots, except that their turbans have peaks or bills. Their arms are also the same with those in general use in Rájpootáná, except that for a long time they considered it disgraceful and a proof of cowardice to carry firearms, and did not carry even a shield with them. Though not numerous themselves, the tribal divisions among them are many, four of whom only are important—namely, the Wálá, the Khachur, and the Khoomán, who are termed "noble," and the Ehwarutiás, who are termed "ignoble," the usages among whom are different in several respects. The chief divinity recognised by all the tribes is the Sun; but they have little sense of religion, and no prayers—their worship consisting simply of looking at the luminary and invoking his favour. They have priests, whose functions, however, are confined to the ceremonies of marriage and *shrád.* Great reliance is placed by them in omens, and much respect shown to persons skilled in divination. Marriages are celebrated by them in the same manner as by the Hindus, with this difference, that, when the bridegroom proceeds to the village of the bride to marry her, his entrance is strongly opposed by her friends, two courses only being left to him—namely, either to force his way in, if he can, or to cry *peccavi*, when he is admitted at once with a small following, the rest of his friends being left in the cold, or taken in after further palaver, after which the usual ceremonies are proceeded with. In times past these fights for a wife were often real trials of strength and courage not unattended with danger; but that character of them has long worn off. The re-marriage of widows is freely permitted and availed of by the Káttis, the widow of an elder brother always becoming the wife of a younger brother, though the widow of a younger brother can never be taken by an elder brother. As a rule, the men are much under the authority of their wives, being more henpecked than any other race in India. Like the other tribes near them, they are very fond of spirituous liquors and opium, and take both to excess; and on festive occasions there is no check to their intoxication, except what their wives may choose to exercise over them.

THE KATTOURIES.

We may also notice in this place the Kattouries, or Kattkuries, who occupy that part of the northern Konkan which lies along the base of the Sáhyádri range, and prepare catechu from the *khyre* tree. They profess to be descended from Rávana, King of *Lanká*, the counterfoil hero of the *Rámáyana*, and are said to have settled in their present quarters when the country was a wilderness. They are nomads in habit, and frequently change their place of residence—without, however, passing beyond the limits of the country they have hitherto possessed. The main tribal divisions among them are four—namely, Helum,

Jádoo, Powár, and Sindhi—the first being considered the most important and respectable, and the last the most degraded, while the third are probably identical with the Powerá Bheels. All the septs are exceedingly indolent and improvident, and, being more or less filthy, live almost as outcasts in the places they occupy, having their residences near, but never within, the villages inhabited by other tribes. During the hot weather and the rains they usually work as labourers, grass-cutters, and firewood-sellers; but at all other times they repair to the jungles to prepare catechu, taking up their residence frequently in the sandy bed of a *nulláh*, where they sleep at night. The catechu is prepared by bits of the *khyre* tree being boiled with water, which is thickened and on being cooled becomes firm. Large sums of money are received by them for the preparation from the merchants; but these are even more easily squandered than earned—after which the usual food of the people consists again, as before, of the coarsest roots and vegetables, and the flesh of such animals and vermin as they can procure, including lizards, rats, jackals, and serpents. They are also much addicted to drink, and will frequently pawn their rags for a dram, and then go naked from want. The men have a squalid and half-starved appearance, and the women are scarcely better looking, but are still said to have great authority over their husbands. Their temper, however, is untractable, which gives rise to much disturbance in the family; and the character of the tribe generally is very low, the men being spoken of as thieves and robbers, and the women unchaste. The religion followed by them is Hinduism, the deities particularly worshipped being Bhairo, Bápdeo, Cheerobá, and Bhaváni.

CHAPTER III.

TRIBES OF RÁJPOOTÁNÁ AND THE INDIAN DESERT.

THE MAIRS AND MEENÁS.

NORTH of the Bombay country, in the Arávulli mountains, live the Mairs and the Meenás, who are supposed to be of the same race, and had a history of their own in the past. The place is called *Mairwárá*, and stands as a rampart of hills, rising from 3000 to 4000 feet above the sea, and measuring a length of about 90 miles and a breadth of from 6 to 20 miles, from Guzerát on one side to near the Jumná on the other. The Mairs claim descent from Prithu Ráj of Delhi, and are therefore not a very old race, having branched out of the Meenás, the primeval denizens of Rájasthán. The story is that a son of Prithu took to himself a girl of the Meenás, and that the children born of the union became the fathers of the Mair tribe, the object aimed at being to establish a Rájpoot descent, even at the expense of legitimacy of birth. The original race was subdivided into five great tribes, that ruled over the whole of Rájpootáná, from the Káli Koh to the Jumná, in great strength and for a long period, during the disturbances of the first Mahomedan dynasties of Delhi, to the mortification of the Rájpoots. Eventually they were ousted from their possessions and driven to the mountains, at about the time when Báber invaded India; but the constant internal dissensions that raged in Rájwárá subsequently gave them incessant opportunities to depredate on the States that surrounded them, and all the efforts of the latter to subdue them were signally unsuccessful. "Where hill joins hill," sung Chund, the Hindu poet-laureate of Delhi, "the Mairs and the Meenás are thronged to oppose the advance of the Choháns;" and they maintained this attitude almost throughout the whole of the Mahomedan era, alternately succumbing and depredating, and always fighting with their Rájpoot suzerains. Their powers of annoying with impunity were based on their habits of life and the locality occupied by them; and the state of the country was then much too troubled for any effectual endeavour being made to reduce them. The ostensible occupation followed by them was that of goatherds; but the herds were usually left to the charge of their boys and old men, while the more able-bodied spent their time, mounted on their diminutive and much-enduring ponies, in marauding, plundering, and murdering. They had more than fifty strongholds, or *kotes*, to operate from; and the haughty Rájpoots were obliged to pay black-mail to them to purchase their forbearance. The detriment to trade became so great at last that the Rájpoot States were forced to combine together to beat up their hills and jungles; but they were not finally reduced till 1820, when their country was occupied by the British army then operating in Rájasthán. Mairwárá had been ceded to the British Government previously by Dowlut Ráo Scindiáh, in 1818; but, the States of Oodypore and Jodhpore having claimed rights over some portions of it at this time, nothing was done in it till the later date mentioned, when its entire management was transferred into British hands. Of the steps then taken to reduce the Mairs into obedience and order the most important was, as in Bheelwárá, the formation of a local corps, which converted the freebooters into soldiers, by whom the rest of the people were forcibly reclaimed. The condition of the country has since been comparatively prosperous, cultivation in it having in particular most enormously increased.

The unmixed or Meená race is now exceedingly rare; but the mixed Mair race is found spread over all the hilly parts of Rájwárá as plentifully as before. Previous to the establishment of the British power among them they used to live generally in concealment among their rugged hills, hardly wearing any clothing, and practising no useful occupation besides herding. Their habits have so far changed that they all put on a loin-cloth and a *chádur* now, after the same fashion as the Bheels; and, the plan of living by plundering only having become obsolete, they have been obliged to become cultivators to a great extent, while some have taken service as soldiers under the paramount power. In their native fastnesses there are, of course, some Mairs yet almost as wild and ferocious as they ever were, who continue to hold the Rájpoots of the plains in utter contempt, and are known all over Upper India principally as dacoits; but even these are coming round gradually, and, having commenced to intermarry with the Rájpoots, are shaping their manners and customs after them. They all profess to be Hindus, with the exception of those who have become Mahomedans, and their marriage and other ceremonies are conducted in Rájpoot fashion; but they are not over scrupulous in the observance of the tenets they profess, and, in the matter of food especially, are not very particular. They eat the flesh of sheep, cows, and buffaloes without hesitation, and even when the animals have died of disease, but refrain from the flesh of hogs and fowls. Strong drinks are also indulged in by them, but very seldom to excess. Two revolting customs had existed long among them—namely, infanticide and the sale of women—which are believed to have since died out. Widow-marriage is very common with them, and also divorce, even more than among the Bheels. If tempers do not agree, or other causes prompt them to part, the husband tears a shred from his turban and gives it to his wife, and, with this deed of separation in her hand, and placing two jars of water on her head, she takes whatever path she pleases, and the first man who chooses to ease her of the jars becomes a new husband unto her. Another peculiarity of the tribe is that they do not tolerate the residence of aliens amongst them, and are necessarily obliged to subdivide themselves into the classes of cultivators, artificers, and servants, having thus their own smiths, carpenters, potters, barbers, *chámárs*, and minstrels. The arms used by the Mairs are the sword, shield, and spear or javelin. Their old rules prohibited them from robbing a Bráhman, a woman, and a *fakir*, and it is said that these are yet rigidly adhered to.

THE DESERT TRIBES.

In the Indian desert lying between Rájwárá and the Indus the principal wild tribes, after the Bheels, Kolis, and Mairs, are the Sodás, Kaorwás, Dháttis, Lohannás, Rebárris, and Sehráes, who may be very shortly described in this place.

THE SODÁS.

The Sodás profess to be of Rájpoot descent, and at one time their power all over the desert border was very great. But they have long lost their original name for courage, and are now chiefly known as dexterous thieves only. Their arms are the sword, the shield, and a long knife worn in the girdle. The primitive sling is also used by them, and with great expertness. Their general condition is very barbarous; but they are rich in herds of camels, oxen, and goats, the milk of which affords them a plentiful and nutritious fare, varied with the flesh of their goats on particular occasions. The jungles of the desert, moreover, yield them wild vegetables of various kinds, and with these comforts they are generally contented and happy.

THE KAORWÁS.

The Kaorwás are nomadic, and have no fixed place to live in. They are constantly moving about with their flocks, and encamp wherever they can find a spring and pasture for them, where they improvise temporary huts for their own accommodation, under some wide-spreading tree, in such skilful manner that the existence of any habitation there cannot easily be detected. Their habits are peaceful, and they are more frequently the victims of outlaws than outlaws themselves. They rear camels, cows, buffaloes, and goats, and sell them to merchants and others; and this is the only occupation they live by.

THE DHÁTTIS.

The Dháttis are very like the Kaorwás—that is, also of pastoral and peaceful habits. They cultivate to a small extent, but so rudely as virtually to leave it to nature to raise the crops. Their supply of food-grains is more certainly acquired by bartering the *ghee* derived from their flocks, which helps them to secure many other necessaries of life also. Their chief fare consists of porridge and buttermilk, and, the cows of the desert being much larger than those of the plains, the produce of three or four cows is sufficient to supply all the requirements of a large family by the sale of *ghee*.

THE LOHANNÁS.

The Lohannás form a numerous tribe, and are principally of commercial habits. They are said to be of Afghán descent, but wear the Bráhmanical string, or *junoee*, and are perhaps the only race of Mahomedans who affect to be Hindus. They conduct the main portion of the traffic between India and the countries beyond the Indus. Their habits are necessarily migratory; but they are otherwise not very wild at present, being apt scribes and shop-keepers. In the matter of food only they are as omnivorous and undiscriminating as any of the other tribes named, not stopping at anything except their cats, dogs, and cows; and they drink spirituous liquors also to an immoderate extent.

THE REBÁRRIS.

The Rebárris are shepherds, goatherds, and camel-breeders, and have a name for stealing camels, in which they are said to be very dexterous. When any of them comes upon a herd of camels grazing, he strikes his lance at the first animal he reaches, and, dipping a cloth with its blood, thrusts it close to the nose of the next animal, and wheeling about sets off at speed, upon which he is pursued by the whole herd, the leader of which is lured by the scent of the blood, and is followed by the rest. The life of the race is almost purely rural, and in general habits they resemble the Sodás more than any other tribe. They have usually many wives; and their women are not ill-looking.

THE SEHRÁES.

The Sehráes are a large race, and have sub-divisions named the Kossál, Chándiá, and Sudáni. They form altogether the principal robber tribe of the desert; and their bands are mostly mounted on horses or camels, and are armed with lances of bamboo and iron, and swords and shields. Of late years they have reduced their modes of rapine to a system, and are content to levy black-mail—paid either in money or grain—for every plough working within their reach; and it is exceedingly difficult to elude them.

THE THORI.

There are many other tribes in the desert, most of whom are of Beloochee descent. One of these, the Thori, have the distinctive epithet of *Bhoot*, or devil, applied to them, and are also called "the sons of the devil." They are so reckless and so entirely destitute of moral sense that they will not hesitate even to bring a man's head to his enemy for the most trifling remuneration; and this is the general character of the rest.

CHAPTER IV.

THE KOLARIAN AND OTHER RACES IN BENGAL.

THE country called Chotá Nágpore terminates the plateau of Central India on the east, and is connected, by a continuous chain of hills, on one side, with the Vindhyá and Kymore ranges, and, on another, with the highlands of Amarkantak. The average elevation of the tract is about 2,000 feet above the sea, and here the Kolarian races, fleeing before their conquerors, seem to have taken their final stand. Of the separate names by which those races were distinguished, the best known now are the Koles and the Sonthâls; but they all formed a kindred people at one time, by whom the Bráhman onset Bengalwards seems to have been most vigorously opposed. They were finally defeated, broken up, and scattered; upon which they settled in different parts of the Chotá Nágpore Division, and in the Tributary Estates of Chotá Nágpore and Cuttack. Alongside of them, but as a distinct race, are found the Oráons, another aboriginal race, who, though not of the Kolarian type, appear to have shared with the Koles the glory of having best resisted the Bráhmans. The story of the Oráons is that they came to Chotá Nágpore after the Koles, agreeing to occupy the place jointly with them without fighting, under the condition of mutual help against a common enemy; and they both differ almost equally in all respects from the people of the plains, at the same time that they are distinguished from one another by features peculiar to each. Their country was a jungle when they came to it; they have converted it into a garden; and the praise is due in the same degree to both.

The Koles.

The Koles are a numerous people, divided into several tribes, among whom are the Moondás, the Larkás, the Hos, the Chooárs, and the Bhoomij. They occupy all the country from the jungles of Rámgurh, near Házáreebágh, to the south and southward, down to the confines of Gángpore and Sirgoojá; but those dwelling in Singbhoom, a portion of which is called the *Koleḣán*, are the best known. The original inhabitants of the Koleḣán were the Bhooyáns, an extremely simple and inoffensive people, who were excellent cultivators and rich in cattle, and by whom the Koles, when they came in, were invited to settle at their side. The two races went on very peacefully together in this state of pristine love till some Márwáree adventurers, journeying through their country, incited the Koles to get up a quarrel with the Bhooyáns, upon which the latter removed themselves to Poráhát, Bonái, and other places lying on the way from Orissá to Behár, where they have become almost completely Hinduised, though still leading the same simple, harmless, and unsophisticated life as before. Where the Koles came from cannot now be very easily explained, for the race is a widely diffused one, of which branches are met with almost in every direction. If they be identical with the Kolis of Western India, or of common descent with them, there is, as was first pointed out by Sir George Campbell, in his *Ethnology of India*, a hiatus of four or five degrees of longitude now between the two septs, caused probably by the Gonds having forcibly intervened between them. Tribes having similar names are also to be found in other places, though the characteristics by which they are severally distinguished are not identical. After their settlement in the Kolehán, the Rájpoots for a long series of years claimed a sort of authority over the Koles, which, however, was never acknowledged by them, and the Rájáh of Chotá Nágpore attempting to enforce it gave rise to the insurrection of 1819-20 in Palámow. There was a second insurrection in 1831, which, originating in Chotá Nágpore, spread rapidly all over the districts of Singbhoom, Rámgurh, Toree, and Palámow; and this also was a rising more against the zemindárs than against the

Government. One general cause of it was the cruelty of the zemindárs, who extorted *ábwábs* (presents) at will, which the Koles were unable to pay easily, severely punishing those who resisted; and another, the transfer of lands from the possession of men descended from the original settlers of the soil to alien proprietors, under a farming lease. A specific case of oppression especially resented was this, that a particular zemindár had given farms of some villages to certain Sikh and Mahomedan adventurers over the heads of the Kole chiefs or *Mánkis*, and that, the latter having been dispossessed, their women were abused and ill-treated. Generally an inoffensive people, the Koles became wild with excitement over this question, and rose in a body to resist. They would not forego their rights, and did not understand the legal quibbles by which those rights were said to have been forfeited. The ill-treatment of their women was naturally another sore point with them, and they assembled together and planned a general revolt. "We have been cheated and dishonoured," said the different tribes to each other; "we are brethren, and must fight together for revenge." Arrows were circulated like the fiery cross among their people in all places, and they rose everywhere to plunder, burn, and kill. A discreet magistrate might have settled matters even at this stage without difficulty; but there was no such officer on the spot. The Koles were opposed as rebels, and, as they showed themselves to be not unworthy of their descent from the hardy *Dasyas* who had resisted the Bráhmans, their whole country had to be swept from one extremity of it to the other before the insurrection could be extinguished. This done, the grievances they complained of were attended to and redressed, by the revenue administration being reorganised so as to restore the Mánkis to authority and deprive the zemindárs of the power to oust them; and since then, by a re-settlement in 1867, the management of the Koleh̄án has been directly assumed by the officers of the Government.

The Koles are a fine people—much finer than the other cognate tribes around them. They are of a black colour, like the rest, and their countenances are not well-favoured; but they are hardy and athletic, have an erect and easy carriage and long free strides, and their hands and feet are both large and well-formed. The hair is worn long, and combed and oiled, alike by the males and the females; but the former shave the forehead, which contributes greatly to their ugliness. Clothing is regarded as a superfluity by them, and even the rich have only a narrow *dhoti* and a *doputtá*, which is gladly thrown by except on state occasions. Of the lower orders the women prefer to go naked, or simply pass the *kopni* between their legs and fasten it before and behind to a string wound round the waist; but those of the higher orders have already taken to tasteful *sárees*, and look handsome in them. In all places the want of clothing hitherto arose mainly from the art of weaving being unknown to them; but this difficulty is being removed by the introduction of foreign weavers into their country. The ornaments worn by the women are ear-rings and immense bunches of bead necklaces, of which they are very fond. The men also wear ear-rings, and necklaces of small beads with charms against snakes, tigers, and diseases depending from them. Their arms are the bow and arrows, and the battle-axe called *tángi;* and in times past they led bloody forays, in which a large amount of violence was committed. At present all their vigour is expended on field-sports, of which they are passionately fond; and among some tribes, such as the Moondás and the Hos, even young boys are trained up as *shikáries*, and are to be seen stalking about birds' nests with bows and arrows. The implements which are now most generally in use, however, among all the tribes are those used in agriculture—namely, the plough, the harrow, the sickle, and the *kodáli* or big hoe; and they plough with cows as well as with bullocks, which is natural to a people making no use of milk. The whole of the Kolchán is extremely fertile and well watered, and three crops of rice are raised in it annually, besides which they cultivate maize, millet, wheat, pulses, mustard, tobacco, and cotton. They take great interest also in farming; and a vast number of sheep, goats, and cattle are bred, and the milk and *ghee* of the cattle are sold in great quantities for the most trifling prices. Ducks, geese, and poultry are also reared, and animal food of all kinds is eaten, beef and hog's flesh included; but, unlike other tribes in their neighbourhood, they do not eat bears, monkeys, field-mice, and snakes. They have no caste prejudices, and eat rice by whomsoever it may be cooked; but they have their own peculiar superstitions, and will leave off eating if a man's shadow passes across the dish, and never drink water from an earthen vessel touched by any other tribe. They are passionately fond of dancing, and have a great variety of dances, which they perform with precision; and little children hardly on their legs begin to learn the dancing-steps. This exhibits them as a light-hearted and good-natured race; but there is another side of the picture which is not equally flattering. They are exceedingly indolent, so much so that their women have to perform all the hardest duties of the field; immoderately dirty, and, except in the hot season, will seldom touch water; and inordinately fond of drink, which accounts for the *soondis* being seen in shoals throughout their country, it being a common saying among themselves that on marriage and other festive occasions they get so drunk that servants forget their duty to their masters, children their reverence for their parents, men their respect for women, and women their respect for decency. They are also extremely sensitive, which makes cases of suicide very common among them. But they are, on the other hand, very manly and honest; and, even when they were living by plunder and violence, lying, deceit, and pilfering were never laid to their charge. The truth of the men and the modesty of their women have, in fact, been always proverbial; and it frequently happens that when a man has committed a crime, far from attempting to conceal it, he comes forward unasked and surrenders himself red-handed for punishment.

The villages of the Koles are of small size and irregular shape, but generally situated prettily on the hills, so as to overlook their flat-terraced rice-fields and undulating uplands. The irregularity in form arises from the houses being distinct from each other, and hedged in by their own little plots of cultivation respectively; and the size is not extensive because of the dislike of the people to congregate from fear ot fires and contagious diseases. The consequence is that almost every crest of ground in the country has been converted into a village, but each consisting of a few scattered huts only. None of the villages are ever built by river sides, and the women have necessarily to draw water from great distances. The houses of the nomad Koles are, for the most part, small and miserable, being temporary, as they are always looking out for fresh clearings in the forests; but those of the stationary tribes, and especially of their chiefs, are always substantial, roomy, and well made, and usually built so as to enclose a square, often having also a verandá to boast of. The compartments are ordinarily three in number—namely, for sleeping, eating, and keeping stores in respectively; and opposite to each house, at a distance of about thirty paces, there is always another for accommodating servants, wayfarers, and guests, the flanks of the two being joined by cow-houses, granaries, and pig-styes. Among the Larkás, the most powerful tribe of all, the unmarried young men are not allowed to sleep in the family-house at night; but this custom is not observed by the Moondás, Hos, and other tribes, among whom all the members of a family live together at all hours. Over love-making and free intercourse there are no restrictions at all. The girls have their prices fixed on them, which their lovers must pay before the consent of their parents to their marriage can be obtained; but no other impediment intervenes, and, if matters go too far between any particular couple, the case is usually settled by the lover being made to pay the girl's price and to marry her. The selection in every case is made by the parties concerned, but has to be finally ratified by their parents as a matter of form. The marriage ceremony is very simple. After everything has been settled, the bride is led to the bridegroom's house and seated on a *morá* of *dhán*, when oil is poured on her head, and boiled rice and meat are offered to her, by partaking of which she becomes of her husband's caste. There is next a dance in the nearest grove, in which the cortège on both sides take part; a cup of beer is then given to each of the lovers, and the liquor of the two cups being mixed is drunk up by both, which completes the rite. After remaining three days with her husband, the most modest course for the wife to follow is to run away from his house and tell her friends that she cannot love him; and the husband must show great anxiety for her, find her out, and carry her back by force, when she becomes settled with him for good. Wives are very well treated by the Koles, and necessarily so, because they work very hard for their husbands. A Kole wife is invariably her husband's companion, and is consulted by him in all his difficulties; and this is especially so among the Hos. She is not subjected to any restraint whatever, and infidelity on her part is very rare. Where it does occur the unfaithful wife is discarded, and her seducer has to refund to her husband the price he paid for her. Polygamy is permitted, but is seldom availed of. The religion of the Koles is based on the belief of a Supreme Being named Sing Bongá, who is represented by the Sun. The Moon is believed to be his wife, and the Stars his daughters. Besides these there are a herd of local and sylvan gods; but of none are images made, nor is any sort of worship known beyond sacrifices. Every village has a grove attached to it where the sacrifices are performed; but the minor gods are propitiated only as intercessors with Sing Bongá. The appeals to them are constant in cases of sickness and for good crops, and the sacrifices are always accompanied by bacchanalian debaucheries. The belief in omens and charms is also great, especially among the tribes on the Sumbulpore frontier, who have mixed much with the Gonds. All the Koles burn their dead on the pyre, with their ornaments, arms, and raiment on. The half-consumed bones are then taken out of the ashes and put into an earthen vessel, which is buried along with rice, clothes, and money, and a stone is placed over the spot; and close to Chyebássá, on the road to Keonjhur, a group of cenotaphs is seen, some of them built with very big stones.

THE SONTHÁLS.

The Sontháls are a nomad race, believed, like the Koles, to have emigrated from the northern parts of India. They occupy all the western jungles of Bengal, particularly those of Rewáh, Palámow, Házáreebágh, Chotá Nágpore, Mánbhoom, and Cuttack; and yet more especially those at the foot of the Rájmahal hills, where the tract inhabited by them is called *Sonthálíá*, or the Sonthál Pergunnáhs. The district lies between Behár and Bengal, and has the shape of an angle doubled by the Ganges as it passes down from the first province into the second. It forms at the present day the most important of all the Sonthál settlements, though it was apparently not one of their original seats, the traditions of the race speaking of it as one of the last places they inhabited in their wanderings. It is subdivided into two distinct parts—namely, an inner territory about 1,400 square miles in extent, which is called the Dámun-i-koh, and a second territory about 4,200 square miles in extent, which surrounds the first, and seems to have been later settled upon. Unlike the Koles, the Sonthâls care little to stick permanently at any particular spot; and, as the Páháriáhs, who inhabit the upper hills of the Dámun, were at all times content with their summits, and repudiated the valleys and the level lands lying beyond them, the Sonthâls came gradually to occupy them, from their fondness for virgin ground. In course of time they increased in numbers on the spot, both by birth and immigration; and, when the clearances effected by them became extensive, the Government was glad to settle the lands with them. The Páháriáhs looked on these advances with distrust, and at one time gave much trouble to their neighbours in consequence; but they have got cured of their predatory habits long since, and the Sonthâls have had no reason to complain of them for many years past. Their later annoyances came rather from the zemindárs and the *mahájuns*, who managed between them to drive the Sonthâls into rebellion in 1854-55. The zemindárs, besides levying their legitimate dues, exacted as much more as they thought their ryots could be made to pay; and, what with *gomástás*, *suburákárs*, peons, and agents, false measures at *hâts* and markets, and the wilful trespass of the rich on growing crops by letting in cattle on them, the system was felt as very oppressive by a simple-hearted people. To meet these extortions, the Sonthál was obliged to have recourse to the *mahájun*, who was ever ready to advance whatever sums were asked for. But the debts thus contracted could never be repaid. Paid ten times over, they still remained unliquidated; and the Sonthál's accounts of knots on a string invariably went to the wall against the account-books produced by the *mahájun* in court in support of his claim. "Do the *Sáhebs*, then, join with the *mahájuns* in cheating and oppressing us?" asked each Sonthál of his neighbour, in alarm. "What alternative is there, then, for us but to rebel?" And they rose in revolt, to resist both the *mahájuns* and the *Sáhebs*. The story of Sidhoo and Kánoo is well known. They proclaimed themselves to be messengers from heaven especially deputed to redress the wrongs of their race; and the Sonthâls gathered around them in large numbers in arms. A police-dárogá, endeavouring to suppress the rising forcibly, was killed by Sidhoo, and, blood having been shed, the rebellion extended rapidly, with frightful atrocity. Troops poured in now into Sonthália from all sides; and, as the Sonthâls would not yield, they had to be shot down in numbers, after which the country was pacified. As in the Kolehán, a more genial administration was now given to it than it had possessed before, whereby the systems of oppression it had suffered from were swept away. From the direct hearing of cases, speedy orders, expeditious appeals, absence of interference on the part of the *ámláh*, etc., the Sontháls felt that their position was now very much bettered, and quietly resumed the peaceful life they had momentarily abandoned. A second rising was threatened in the outer tract on a later day, on account of the rack-renting practised there by the zemindárs and ghátwáls; but this was averted by the jungles of the tract being resumed by the Government, and the entire area of the Sonthál Pergunnáhs resettled on the ryotwary system—that is, with the Sontháls.

The Sonthál is absolutely the best specimen of the wild tribes in India. He is a short, well-made, and active man, having a round face, and the thick lips, high cheek-bones, and spread nose of the Gond, Bheel, and Kole. He is beardless—or nearly so—while the hair of his head is straight, coarse, and black. In his dealings with other men he is shy, if not cowardly; but he is very brave when confronted with wild animals. He is a good hunter, a good herdsman, and a good agriculturist; self-dependent in everything and never idle, and necessarily almost never in distress. His skill, patience, and diligence are exemplary; and he has implements of his own making and a peculiar system of cultivation which enable him to cultivate very successfully, after his own manner. He always reclaims the jungles he comes to inhabit, and carefully collects all their products, which he either sells or barters for other articles from his neighbours; but he will do all this for himself and his family only, and will never take service with any one. If any attempt be made to coerce him he never thinks of offering resistance, but decamps into the innermost jungles, where it is impossible to follow him, and where he commences new clearances on his own account. Like the Kole, he is not a weaver himself, but he has had weavers about him from a longer date, and usually dresses better than the Kole, though his working dress is often none other than the *kopni*, or cloth passed between the legs and fastened to a string worn round the loins. His wife makes a more decent appearance at all times. She is short like her husband, and plump, but has usually a pleasing expression in her countenance; and her dress for many years past has been the Bengali *sáree*, which she wears in the same fashion as the Bengalis, except that no part of it is used as a veil. The chief ornaments in use among both sexes are flowers and feathers, and also cowtail-hair necklaces, which are very neatly manufactured. The women also wear on their arms, ankles, and throats ornaments made of brass and bell-metal, which are excessively heavy; and the love of the husband is in this sense a sore burden to the wife. The food of the Sonthál consists principally of *janerá* and maize, accompanied with eggs, poultry, and the flesh of goats, kids, or swine; but he will eat anything besides that he can obtain, and is not particular as to the hands they come from, with one singular exception only. His antipathy against the Hindu is so great that he will never eat cooked food coming even from the hands of a Bráhman, though there is no tradition to account for the feeling, which has come down to him from generation to generation, testifying to the existence of some bitter feud between the races in the past. The chief drink of the Sontháls is the *pachwái*, or fermented grain; but they do not drink so much as the Koles, and their debauch is necessarily less to that extent.

Though he is but a nomad in habits, the hut of the Sonthál is well made, and well raised. Its walls are made of matting, or hurdle, or thin sticks smeared over with mud; and, owing to his love of colours, a gay appearance is often given to them by their being painted with different shades of red, white, and black, according to the owner's fancy. The roof is of thatch, and every hut is always roomy within, the Sonthál having usually a large family to accommodate. Each couple has an average of eight or nine children, and the house is necessarily always full; but it is also always clean, and has a tidiness in almost everything about it. The arrangement of houses is such as to form a long street through every village, one house deep on each side; and each house has attached to it a pig-sty and a dove-cot, besides which there are buffalo-sheds scattered here and there, varying in size according to the wealth of the inhabitants. The villages are buried in thick jungle, but are not difficult to find, being easily traceable by the small cleared patches of ground to be found near them, which are always pleasant to look at, and yet more by the music proceeding from them at all times. The Sonthál is an admirer of nature, and never fells down any useful or ornamental tree, which gives his clearings a park-like and unmistakable appearance; and he is Arcadian in practice, and enjoys life better than other people of the same grade, from being immensely fond of music and dancing. His flute is a simple instrument made of the bamboo, but gives out deep, rich tones; and every village has a dancing-ground where the youths and maidens meet in the evening to dance and sing. This is the national custom, and no harm is thought of it; and the maidens, decked with flowers and feathers, pair off with the young men, all blithely going round in a circle, with their feet falling in cadence, and singing responsive to musicians placed in their centre. That such freedom of intercourse may not be abused, there is a *jág-mánjee*, or censor, in every village, to look after the morals of the young, while another officer superintends all family arrangements generally, and, with the aid of the village priest, keeps matters straight. There is a covered platform besides in each village, where the head men meet to talk over and regulate village affairs, and to award punishments where they may have been deserved. All marriages in the Sonthál country are said to be love-matches, though it is considered respectable for the parents to mature the necessary arrangements, as if without the knowledge of the lovers. The selection is said to be preceded by a beastly festival, named *Bandana*, which is held in the month of January, and lasts for six days, when all candidates for matrimony, male and female, are assembled together and permitted to have promiscuous intercourse with each other, each lover selecting his future wife after the termination of this general carnival. Polygamy is permitted, but is seldom had recourse to; and the wife is always treated with kindness. Divorces are also permitted when man and wife find out that they are not suited to each other, the order of separation being invariably given by a *punchâyet*.

The tribal divisions of the Sonthâls are: the Saran, Murmu, Márli, Kisku, Besárá, Hánsdá, Tudi, Báski, Hemroo, and Chorái; but they do not materially differ from each other in any respect. The chief god of all the tribes is Sing Bongá, the same as of the Koles; and he is worshipped after the same fashion also, namely, as the Sun God. Besides him there are several minor gods and *bhoots* who have to be propitiated; and the spirit of Borá Mánjee, a deceased and canonised chief, is also venerated, and often invited by the initiated, by fasting and sacrifices, to answer references made to it in respect to village affairs. The Bágh-Bhoot, or tiger spirit, is another object of reverence; and several tribes worship the living tiger as well as the *bhoot*. The women pay great respect likewise to the elephant, and touch the earth with their foreheads before him, praying him to bless their children, who are seated in perfect confidence at his feet. Of set celebrations one of the greatest is the hunting festival organised annually, which every adult has to join fully armed and accoutred. The arms of the Sonthâls are the same as of the Gonds, Bheels, and Koles—namely, the battle-axe, and the bow and arrows; and with these they go out to hunt in a body, pursuing wild animals of all kinds, except tigers and bears, which are never wantonly molested, though, if their path be crossed by either, they are not afraid to encounter them. The expedition lasts for four or five days, after which the game secured enables the party to celebrate a great feast, which the women are invited to join. Feasts on smaller scales are also celebrated on occasions of marriages and deaths. The dead among the Sonthâls are burnt, as among the Koles; but the ashes and bones, instead of being buried, are consigned to the currents of rivers held sacred after the Hindus.

THE ORÁONS.

The Oráons, better known as the Dhángurs, or hill-men, inhabit the north and west parts of the Chotá Nágpore district, and are also scattered over the other districts of the division, and over Sumbulpore. They have a tradition among them that they came originally from Konkan, and settled first at Rhotás, whence one party diverged to their present quarters, while another party, the Páháriáhs, occupied the Rájmahal hills. When they came to Chotá Nágpore the Koles of the Moondá tribe were already settled in it; but, being of a peaceful disposition, these offered no opposition to them, and the two races lived side by side in harmony together. As the Hindus spread and prevailed the Oráons were obliged to fly before them, and came thus to be diffused over all the country now occupied by them. The plateau of Chotá Nágpore which they inhabit is a magnificent place; but their life and appearance are not in keeping with the scenery. They are small-sized and ill-favoured; and, though their young men give themselves a jaunty air and are very careful in decorating their persons, that does not exhibit them to greater advantage. They are of dark complexion, and have projecting jaws and thick lips, while their forehead is low and narrow, and their eyes are meaningless and vacant. The hair is worn long, and gathered into a knot behind, which supports a red or white turban on gala days; but ordinarily there is a mirror and a comb stuck into it, with bright buttons and chains having spiky pendants dangling therefrom. Here the decorations of the Oráons end, and even these are discarded after marriage, which makes their subsequent appearance unprepossessing and negligent. The only cloth worn by them is a narrow strip wound round the loins, and in the wilder parts of the country even this is wanting, the *kopni*, or cloth passed between the legs, being substituted for it. The men are, however, always very good-humoured, and the women modest in demeanour, though their dress, too, is scanty. In some places the women have the usual *sáree* with red border, which serves as a petticoat, and even a *chádur* to put over the body; but in others the bandage round the loins is their only clothing—worn longer, however, than by the men. The ornaments of the women consist of a large quantity of red beads and heavy brass necklaces hung round the throat, and rings of copper on the fingers and in the ears, besides which they are tattooed all over the body—on the forehead, arms, and back—even young men bearing the marks on their forearms. One sign of civilisation is certainly shown by the women: they wear false hair to make up with their natural hair a chignon of size, over which heron plumes are displayed on festive occasions. Another test of civilisation (native) is that the *soi-pátána* of Bengali women is understood by them, and is named *gui*. When two girls feel a particular penchant for each other they swear eternal friendship and exchange necklaces, and the compact is witnessed by common friends. They do not name each other after this ratification of goodwill, but are "my flower," or "my *gui*," or "my meet-to-smile," to each other to the end of their lives.

The huts of the Orάons are badly built and huddled up, and are quite incapable of affording decent accommodation; and the consequence is that the men and their cattle live, not only within the same compound, but often in the same apartment. The walls of the huts are of mud, and where constructed of red laterite earth are as durable as if built of brick and mortar. The accommodation being scanty, the young members of a family do not live with their parents, the bachelors of the village having a hall common to themselves, while the maidens are billeted with the widows, who, if not discreet, often allow them to mix freely with their lovers. The bachelors' hall has a dancing arena before it, where young men and girls meet frequently to amuse themselves; and, during the festive seasons, they often dance throughout the night, provided the supply of beer is sufficient to keep up the enjoyment so long. As a rule, however, boys and girls of the same village do not intermarry, it being considered more respectable to bring home a bride from a distance. The marriage of children is unknown;

and, as among the Sonthāls, most of the marriages are said to be love matches purely. The selection of his wife is always made by the would-be husband himself, after which his parents go through a form of selection for him. When the time for the marriage is settled, the bridegroom, with a party, proceeds to the bride's village to bring her over; but she is not surrendered before a mock fight with her friends, who refuse to part with her. The fight eventually ends in a dance, in which the bride and bridegroom join. The marriage ceremony is called *sindoordán*, and is performed under a screen. The bride and bridegroom are made to stand over a curry-stone, the former being posted before the latter, and both surrounded by their friends, while all intruders are turned out. A cloth is then thrown over them, and the man daubs the girl's head with *sindoor*, or vermilion, while the girl returns the compliment by just touching his brow without turning her head. They are then bathed, and retire to a private apartment to change their clothes, from which they come out sometime after, and are saluted man and wife. Both man and wife live as labourers, and the race is widely known as the chief labouring class of Bengal. Many of them go out as emigrant coolies to various parts of the world, and return with money enough to maintain them in independence if they could only husband their savings properly. But this they never can; they spend in a month what would make them comfortable for life, and then cheerfully return to work and privations. They believe that they were created for labour, and have a natural relish for it. Their work is enlivened with sports, and the men are quite as fond of field sports as the Moondás and the Hos, and are very successful hunters. Whatever they hunt they eat; but their chief food is rice and *dál.* They seldom use vegetables, and their cooking is so wretched that they could not possibly have made anything eatable out of them. Their religion, like that of the Koles and the Sonthháls, recognises a Supreme God who is made manifest in the Sun; but they think it useless trouble to pray to him, as he does not send evil. There are malignant spirits who afflict mankind, and these have to be propitiated, since even the Sun-God cannot control them, or protect any one from their persecutions. The belief in ghosts, sorceries, and witchcrafts is also widely diffused; and there are two important functionaries in each village—the Maháto and the Páhn, or the secular administrator and the priest—whose chief duty is to look after and regulate the precautionary measures to be taken. They have no idea of futurity. Men killed by tigers become tigers, but for all others death is annihilation, excepting those who, dying under peculiar circumstances, become ghosts. The dead are burned, and the ashes and charred bones being collected are placed in an earthen vessel, which is kept suspended near the house of the deceased till the cold weather, when its contents are allowed to mix with the bones and ashes of his ancestors. The chief festivals of the Oráons are two, and both of them are agricultural—namely, the *Sarhul* festival, which solemnises the marriage of the earth, and the *Karma* festival, which celebrates a plentiful harvest.

THE PÁHÁRIÁHS.

The Rájmahál hills, we have said, are occupied by two distinct races—namely, the Páháriáhs, who inhabit the summit of the hills, and the Sontháls, who live at their foot and in the valleys. The hillmen are the original inhabitants, the Sonthâls the interlopers; and the latter were frequently depredated upon by the former in times gone by. The character of the hillmen was utterly savage and cruel, and throughout the Mahomedan period they were the scourge and terror alike of the Sonthâls and the surrounding country, while the zemindárs of the plains encouraged their predatory habits by employing them against each other. They accordingly lived by rapine; and not only was the neighbourhood of the hills and the roads traversing them unsafe, but so was the passing of boats by the Ganges. This continued to be the case even for a long time after the establishment of the English power; and the Government dák-runners were frequently murdered and their wallets plundered. Troops were sent to chastise the offenders; but the jungles on their hills were impervious, and there were no roads besides stony and steep footpaths by which to come up to them. The Mahomedans had encountered the same difficulty in their day, and had left the hillmen uninterfered with; but the English Government was determined to subdue them, and eventually succeeded in doing so by tact and kindness. This new policy was introduced by two young Captains of the East India Company's army, named Brooke and Brown, who invited and feasted the hill-chiefs and their dependents in their camps, and then sent them home with presents of turbans, beads, and other similar trifles. The act awakened a new feeling in their minds, which was promptly availed of by Mr. Cleveland, a young civilian, who was then the judge and magistrate of Bhaugulpore. He visited the savages in their own hills, unarmed and almost alone, distributing presents to and feasting hundreds of them at a time; and they were by these means induced, first, to come to a parley, and, eventually, to a definite understanding with the Government, which has always been respected by them. There were some disputes afterwards between them and the zemindárs at the foot of the hills, in respect to boundaries and the rights of wood and grazing; upon which the hill-territory was, in 1832, separated from the plains, demarcated, and, with every right re-acquired from the zemindárs, made over to the hillmen rent-free, on the sole condition of good behaviour, which they have faithfully observed. Even the Sonthåls are no longer interfered with by them, so long as they do not attempt to ascend their hills, the two races occupying their respective allotments seemingly without any knowledge of each other.

The Pâháriáhs are shorter in size even than the Sonthåls, and also of slighter make; but their frames are well knit and their limbs finely turned; and they have always been very adventurous and brave. They are of a fair complexion, and have broad faces, small eyes, and flattish, up-turned noses; and their women are pretty, and have good figures. The men are very fond of dandyism, and oil and comb their hair carefully, and tie it up in a knot on the head, passing two long locks over the ears. Over the knot a red turban is sometimes worn, their only other clothing being a *dhoti* worn round the loins. The women are dressed in skirts of white, and have each a square of gay-coloured tusser silk which is passed over the right shoulder and under the left, and tucked under the skirt at the waist. They also wear coral necklaces, but no metal ornaments beyond rings and chains. The principal tribal divisions of the race are three—namely, the Malers, Máls, and Kumárs; of whom the first retain more of the habits of their ancestors than the other two. The Malers occupy the heights of the Dámun, while the heights of the southern or Rámgurh hills are occupied by the

Máls and the Kumárs, who differ from the Malers in several essential respects, through having fraternised largely with other races. The Máls, for instance, are very fond of dancing, like the Koles and the Sonthâls, and of social enjoyments generally; but the Malers are of a less cheerful disposition and never dance. The former, again, are more particular in the matter of food, having so far picked up Hindu prejudices that they will not eat beef, nor any food not cooked by themselves; but the latter are bound by no such restrictions, and eat anything that they can procure. The staple food of all tribes consists of maize, *janerá*, and beans, which are mainly raised on the table-land and slopes of their hills; but every other necessary of life has to be obtained by them from the plains, by bartering their bamboos, grass, and timber, all of which grow in great profusion on the hills. The crops are all raised by the women, and the process of cultivation is of the simplest kind, the only instrument used being an iron-shod staff, or pointed stick, with which holes are made on the hill-side, at a distance of a foot from each other, into which a mixture of seeds is thrown—namely, of the crops intended to be raised. The men are industrious after their own manner: they will submit to any privations to have a shot at a deer, or to secure a peacock; roam over the forests for many miles in search of honeycombs, wild yams, and gums; manufacture their bedsteads and sowing staffs; bring down to the plains for sale wood, charcoal, bamboos, cotton, and honey; but they will not stoop to clear the hill-side, or to cultivate. Here the women intervene, and offer assistance loyally: "I will do what you won't," says the wife to her lord; and who can help loving such a wife?

The villages of the Páháriáhs have generally a rather civilised appearance, being surrounded by gardens and cultivation-patches. Though they are very dirty in person themselves, their houses and grounds are always kept free from filth and bad smells. The huts are all carefully built of wattled bamboos, no mud whatever being used in their construction; and there are always numerous out-houses for holding grain, pigs, etc. As among several other of the wild races we have noticed, the unmarried adults of both sexes are excluded from the family residence, the males clubbing together to occupy a bachelors' hall, while the females are put into distinct cells provided for them. The intercourse between the sexes, however, is not much restricted, and the lads and lasses are always to be seen romping and love-making, every facility being given to them to do so, for the race is naturally amorous, though the lovers do not necessarily misbehave. The fear of being outcasted is very great, since no one can be re-admitted into society till after expensive sacrifices; and this keeps things straight till the marriage knot is tied. The process followed in getting united is very simple. After selection has been made and approved, the bridegroom goes for the bride to her father's house; and, as soon as the father has joined their hands together, the young man marks the head of the girl with *sindoor* with his right-hand little finger, and then, linking the same finger with the little finger of her right hand, leads her out of the house to his own, while all the party entreat him to be kind and loving to her. One of the most significant admonitions to him on the occasion is that he must not murder her, and this is accompanied by an explanatory note that if she dies a natural death, or by means of the devil, he would not be held responsible for it. Polygamy is allowed and practised, the value of female labour being great; and usually one man has no less than four wives. Widow-marriage is also permitted, and when a man dies his brothers marry up all the widows, as they cannot afford to let them go out of the family. The dead are buried. The religion of the Páhári áhs recognises a Supreme Being, who is named Budo Gossáin, and is represented by the Sun, with other gods under him, each village having a tutelary deity of its own. The Supreme God created seven brothers, they say, to possess the earth; and they pretend to be descended from the eldest of them. Their belief in evil spirits is so great that a long bamboo is fixed in the ground in front of every house to ward off their influence. The belief in the transmigration of souls and in a future state is also general. One peculiar custom of theirs is for the priest to declare truths respecting the future by an interpretation of his own dreams. He affects to be inspired by fits of madness, when he lives apart from all others in the depths of forests and jungles, and receives, or manufactures, the dreams he interprets. This curious imposition apart, the Páháriáhs never deceive or lie. Oaths are taken on the arrow, or on two arrows fixed on the ground with a little salt placed between them, and never are such engagements violated. Their one great sin is drunkenness, the beverage in general use being the *pachwái*, the same that is so well loved by the Sonthàls. In all other respects they have been much reclaimed from the barbarism that belonged to them at one time, and are now usefully employed in several capacities; but it is believed that they are declining in vigour, and gradually dying out.

MINOR TRIBES IN BENGAL.

Apart from the races named above, there are several minor tribes located in the wilds between Bengal and Behár, and between Bengal and Cuttack, and also to the west of Chotá Nágpore, the population of which places is almost wholly aboriginal. The reason why more such races are found in these localities than in any other part of India seems to be that they were driven to them as to an extremity by the successive tides of conquerors by whom they were pursued, there being no securer spot to fly to, since these are all quite impervious for military operations. Besides the races already spoken of and their subdivisions, we accordingly find here: the Bhárs, the Cheroos, the Kanjhars, the Náts, the Thároos, the Kárwárs, the Puttooás, and the Sours, of whom the first and the second are not tribes of sufficient importance or number at present to require further notice here, the bulk of both having intermingled with the more powerful communities about them, while the third and the fourth are cognate tribes of the vagabond race, best known as the gipsies, who will be referred to hereafter in connexion with the wild tribes of the south, as also will be the Thároos along with the frontier races occupying the Terái, where they reside in greater numbers.

THE KÁRWÁRS.

Of the rest, the principal seat of the Kárwárs is Sirgoojá, whence they extend in one direction to Palámow, and in another to Rewáh, while to the direct north they approach the borders of Mirzápore and Benáres. They are a dark, savage-looking people, strongly-built and active, but short-legged; better-looking, however, than the Oráons and the Gonds. Though more hirsute than their cognates they never cultivate their hair or beards, which gives to their coarse features a wilder expression. They live in detached hamlets rather than in villages, for even among themselves they cannot agree to live together except in very small clusters. Their women are excessively hard-worked, and are stunted in growth, black, ugly, and wretchedly clad, having all the burdens of life imposed on them without any of the privileges belonging to their sex. The men may be idling all day, but the women must cultivate and work, hew wood and bring water. They always cultivate newly cleared ground, and for that purpose change their homestead every two or three years. The crops grown are rice, millet, yams, chillies, pumpkins, cucumbers, and arrowroot; but the yield is not very considerable in any case. They are put to no straits, however, on that account, for they have as sure a knowledge of what is edible among the jungle-produce as the monkey; and, on failure of their usual food-supply, easily find out something else to live upon. They know how to smelt iron, and trade in it, and also in honey, beeswax, resins, gums, and sticklac. They do not know aught of Sing Bongá or any other god, and worship nothing, but they sacrifice to their ancestors. One sept of them, the Khurriáh Kárwárs, have been partially Hinduised, and occasionally worship an idol named Khurriáh Ráni, a bloodthirsty goddess like Káli, to whom buffaloes in large numbers are sacrificed. Another sept are the Bhogtáhs, who are prominently distinguished as being more lazy and unimprovable than all the rest.

THE PUTTOOÁS.

The Puttooás, or Mangás, are scattered over the Tributary Mehals of Cuttack, particularly over Keonjhur, Pál Leyrá, and Dhenkenál. Their forms are slight, and their physique seemingly weak. The men are far from being handsome, while the women are decidedly ugly, being a shade more frightful even than those of the Kárwárs. The dress of the men ordinarily is that of the Ooryáh peasantry about them; but the women wear no clothes, their sole covering being two large bunches of leaves, of which one is worn in front and the other behind, both being kept in position by a string of beads passed twenty or thirty times round the loins. It is from this original costume that the tribe has acquired the name of *Puttooá*, or the leaf tribe. They have no covering for the upper part of the person, but the females wear necklaces of different colours which hang down to their waists. For the origin of their sylvan attire they have different legends, which agree in representing it as a punishment inflicted on them by a *Rishi*, or by Devi herself, for their pride in having been originally much given to fine clothes! And the penalty of abandoning the dress imposed on them is, they believe, that they would be eaten up by tigers. Within the last few years a supply of clothing has, from time to time, been distributed among them by the Government, and they have consented to wear it; or at least the men have come to an engagement to that effect on behalf of their women. They are equally rude in other respects, and neither own lands nor cultivate, though they are not undisposed to assist others in cultivating. Their principal pursuit is the chase, and they use their bow and arrows with dexterity, killing deer, hogs, and snakes. They eat everything except the cow; but their usual food consists of roots and seeds of jungle grass. They affect to be Hindus; but no Hindu, however low his caste may be, will agree to eat or mix with them. Their religion consists of the worship of nameless spirits that are believed to inhabit their woods and mountains. Marriages among them are arranged by parents, and give occasion to much revelry and drunkenness, the festivities continuing for three days. The ceremony consists in the thumbs of the pair being tied together by a thread, which typically expresses their union through life.

THE SOURS.

The Sours are chiefly found in the jungles of Khoordá, from Bánpoor to Cuttack, and in the woods which skirt the hills some way to the north of the Mahánadi. They are of very inferior stature and mean appearance, and are jet black in colour;

but they are in general harmless and peaceable, though entirely destitute of moral sense, being very like wild men of the woods. Some of them live in villages, which are called *sais*, and find employment with the zemindárs in clearing jungles and bringing fuel, besides which they also collect the produce of their woods, which they sell in the neighbouring bazárs. Others lead a purely migratory life, wandering from spot to spot, where they erect temporary huts of sticks, leaves, and grass, and clear the ground for raising the grains they live upon, for the year only. They eat almost everything they can come at, and many of them have often nothing better to subsist upon than roots and jungle-berries. Their one constant arm is the axe; but it is used only in felling trees.

CHAPTER V.

TRIBES OF THE MADRÁS PRESIDENCY.

THE KHONDS.

THE Khonds are the principal aborigines of the Eastern Gháts, their country extending from the eastern limit of Gondwáná to the Bay of Bengal, and from the Mahánadi river on the north to the Godávery on the south. A great part of this territory is excessively hilly, and the central table-land has an elevation of about 2,000 feet above the sea. Some portions of the plateau are perfectly bare of wood, but others are covered with trees; and at the foot of it are impenetrable bamboo forests, which grow closer and resist the axe better than every other species of vegetation. The Khond districts are situated both in the plateau and the forests, and belong mainly to the Madrás Presidency, though running also into the dependencies of both Bengal and the Central Provinces. The proper name of the country is *Khondestán;* but a large portion of it is subject to the zemindárs of Goomsur and Chinná Kimedy on one side, and of Boád and

Duspullá on another, the Khonds inhabiting the mountain ranges only, in nominal subjection to the zemindárs. Much was therefore not known of this people before the Goomsur Rebellion of 1836-37, when the British troops ascended the Gháts in pursuit of the Rájáh of Goomsur, who, failing in his feudatory obligations, had defied the paramount power and fled to the Khonds for protection. The Rájáh died shortly after, committing his family to the care of the Khonds; and the Khonds, refusing to give up their guests, became amenable to the penalties of rebellion. They were not unfriendly towards the British Government at the outset, but, being goaded on by the representations of the people of Goomsur, resolved subsequently to repel force by force, which led to a harassing and miserable war, in which they were shot down like wild beasts, and their villages laid in ashes. They were finally compelled to submit, at the same time that the widow and son of the Rájáh of Goomsur were captured; and the first war with them was thereby terminated. But fresh complications were developed within a few years after, or as soon as their strange social organisation came to be understood. The British Government was surprised to find that the wild inhabitants of the Gháts were in the habit of offering human sacrifices to their gods, and also of systematically destroying their female children. It insisted on both the customs being abandoned, and there was a fresh war on the Khonds refusing to comply. As on the first occasion, however, they soon found that it was useless to resist, and, seeing no other way of getting over the difficulty, made whatever promises were demanded of them. It is doubtful if either of the practices objected to has been altogether discontinued even now in the wilder parts of their country impervious to the influence of the Government. This at least is certain, that the humanity which ordered their abolition has not anywhere been appreciated. The Khonds were permitted, at their own request, to denounce the British Government to their gods as the real cause of their apostasy, and, as the gods made no objection to transfer their wrath in the direction indicated, the Khonds have accepted their falling off from the faith of their ancestors as an inevitable evil. But it cannot yet be said truly that they have got reconciled to the change.

The Khonds are a wilder race even than the Gonds and the Bheels as they are now to be seen, and have as yet resisted all efforts made to civilise them. The men are well formed, of a good height, good-looking, and remarkably active; but the women are short in stature and very plain. In colour they are all much fairer than the Gonds, but varying in hue from that of copper to yellowish olive. In the upper elevations both sexes, for the most part, go naked, and, when pinched by cold, alleviate its excess by making fires, while, when the heat of the weather becomes oppressive, they seek shelter under the shade of large trees. The only covering worn by the men in the lower elevations is a coarse cloth wound round the loins, in such a manner as to make the end hang down behind as low as the flaps of a coat, while the head-dress is formed by the hair being rolled up like a horn and then covered with a piece of red cloth decorated with feathers. The lower dress of the women in the same places is nearly like that of the men, with the addition of a gayer fringe; but it rarely descends under the knee, and there is no covering whatever for the upper part of the body. The ornaments in use are brass rings worn on the ear by both sexes, and also on the nostrils by women; the latter likewise wearing necklaces, armbands, and anklets either of brass or of coloured beads. The arms of the men are a long staff, or, in lieu of it, an axe with the blade in two divisions, a sling, and the bow and arrows, the military dress also including a covering of leather or bear's skin for the breast, and a showy crest of cock's feathers on the head. All the Khonds are trained to the use of their weapons from their earliest years, and are especially dexterous in handling the sling and the axe. Like other wild tribes in general, they are constantly at feud, either among themselves or with their neighbours; and on these and similar occasions they march to battle in what they consider to be a very impressive manner, singing and shouting, and always under the influence of strong potations. The different tribes fight with each other on the merest trifle; but one of their remarkable customs is that, as soon as the fighting is terminated, the women pass over from both sides to condole with each other on the loss of their nearest and common relatives. The general peace occupation of the race is agriculture, which is followed with great skill and energy, the result being that they are surrounded by every form of rural affluence. Rice of several sorts, millet, pulses, oils, tobacco, turmeric, and mustard are all grown on the hills; and the surplus stores of them are exchanged with the Brinjáris, or at fairs, for salt, cloth, and brass utensils and ornaments. They have also large herds of buffaloes and cattle of small breed, numerous flocks of goats, and abundance of swine and poultry. Of handicraft they know almost nothing, and indeed affect to despise it; but their huts are nevertheless well made, and are superior to those of the people living below the Gháts. Their general knowledge is very inconsiderable, for they will not submit to learn anything. Even the Gonds, we have seen, have been partially humanised by their contact with the Brinjáris; but no similar result has yet been obtained among the Khonds. Till recently the value of money was not understood by them, and up to this day barter among them, as among the Gonds, is chiefly in kind. Their language, like that of the Gonds, is peculiar to themselves, and is not understood even by their nearest lowland neighbours. Among the agreeable features in their character are: their love of independence, bravery, hospitality, and industry; while the qualifying traits of it include vindictiveness, ferocity, and inordinate debauch.

The primary divisions or classes among the Khonds are three—namely, the Maliáhs, or highlanders, who were originally independent of the zemindárs, and to this day pay no tribute to them; the Benniáhs, who occupy the outskirts of the hills and pay rents for the lands they hold, or account for it by service at their choice; and the Bhetiáhs, a servile class who hold lands on the condition of labour only. The administrative arrangements among all of them are the same, and indeed are based on local divisions of villages and districts, the chiefs, who are always selected for their deeds of valour, being of two sorts—namely, the village chiefs, whose jurisdiction is limited, and the district or superior chiefs, who exercise greater powers. The village chief in Chinná Kimedy is called Mánjee; in Goomsur, Mulliko; and in Boád, Khonro; while the district chiefs are called Bissoees in some places, and Páthurs in others. There is another officer in every village, named Digáloo, or minister, the best spokesman among the villagers being always selected for the post; and it is his duty to regulate the public meetings and assemblies of the people. These meetings are purely democratic, and even women are allowed to attend them, though they are not permitted to take part in the discussions except among particular classes. As a rule the women are not trusted with any affair of importance till it has been separately sat upon. "They *may* betray counsel," say the Khonds, "though the youngest stripling who can bear an axe will never blab of what has been confided to him." For the head of a family all the tribes have the greatest respect, it being a proverb with them that "A man's father is his God on earth." The social organisation among them is indeed strictly patriarchal, the father of a family being its absolute ruler in every case. Disobedience to him under any circumstances is regarded as a crime, and, even when the children are separately lodged, the board is one, for no Khond will ever venture to mess apart from his parents. In their dealings with each other they are usually very faithful, but only within tribal limits. Beyond those limits they are almost as much robbers and spoilers to each other as to strangers. No man can approach a Khond village without being invited to enter it; but, once in, he becomes a guest, and cannot be turned out, and the murderer is safe even among the children of the murdered. The ordinary food of the Khond is *Khichree*, or rice and *dál* boiled together; but the hunters eat freely of game. They draw no milk from their domestic animals, but eat flesh of all kinds, except of dogs, cats, and beasts of prey. Their love of liquor and tobacco is excessive, and the cultivation of tobacco among them occupies a large area. The liquors drunk are of different kinds—namely, those distilled from rice, the *mohowá* flower, and the fruit of the *áppá* tree respectively. A palm peculiar to their country also yields toddy, which is pleasant when fresh, but exceedingly intoxicating in a fermented state. They are fond, too, of dançing, and there is a place set apart for this amusement in every village. The dance is accompanied by music, and the performers are of both sexes. The men have a separate war dance, when they are armed to the teeth and lavishly decorated with red cloth and feathers; and also another dance, which represents a bison-hunt. On both these occasions the battle-axe is brandished as an accompaniment to the dancing, while in the other dances generally the only accompaniment is that of the pipe.

The appearance of a Khond village is rather picturesque, it being usually situated either by a clump of trees, or at the base of a wooded hill, or on the knoll of a valley. It consists of some forty or fifty houses, all built on one uniform model, like the cells of a beehive, the patrician and the plebeian being lodged precisely alike. The number of apartments in each house is three, of which the central room is the family dwelling-place, while the other two rooms are appropriated as a cooking-room and store-room respectively. The bachelors of the village, as among the Gonds, Sonthâls, and Páháriáhs, have a separate house assigned to them; and the maidens also, as with the Oráons, have their distinct quarters, though chastity is not a Khond virtue, and the separation of the young people is not very strictly enforced. All the Khond tribes intermarry; but, reversing the usage prevailing in other places throughout India, boys of ten and twelve are married to girls of fifteen and sixteen. The marriage arrangements are completed by the parents of the parties to be united, and generally in the following fashion:—The father of the bridegroom pays from twenty to thirty head of cattle to the father of the bride as the price of his daughter-in-law, engaging that her chief duty would be to act as a domestic servant in his house. A quantity of rice and liquor are then brought forward, and a libation is poured out to the gods, after which the high contracting parties join hands and declare the contract completed. A feast and a drinking bout follow, in the midst of which the bride is carried off, either on the back of the bridegroom, if he be up to her weight, or by some other person acting on his behalf, to give the affair the semblance of abduction, while all the young women of the bride's party follow the ravisher, and pelt at and abuse him, till he gains the bridegroom's house, when his assailants return home laughing and jubilant. Concubinage is not considered dishonourable by the Khonds, and an unmarried woman is not disgraced by becoming a mother; though, of course, people are not over anxious to marry her. Women have also the right to quit their husbands at pleasure; and this right is availed of among all the tribes—among some as many as eight or ten times. The parents on such occasions have to return the prices that were paid for their daughters, and the trouble and vexation this gives rise to causes a married daughter to be regarded as a curse. The dead among the Khonds are burnt, but without any rite or ceremony, except that the burning of the body of a chief is accompanied by the beating of drums and gongs.

The religion of the Khonds consists of the worship of the Sun and the Earth, the former under the name of Burá Pennu, or Belá Pennu, and the latter under the name of Tárá Pennu. There are six or seven subordinate deities besides—namely, of rain, spring, wealth, the chase, war, boundaries, and judgment; while a third class of gods comprises the descendants of human beings who resisted evil in life, and are believed to preside over villages, hills, streams, fountains, tanks, houses, and forests. The Meriáh sacrifices in Goomsur and Boád were to the Earth-goddess alone, under the effigy of a peacock, and were made under the belief that the process of fertilisation could only be facilitated by drenching the sterile soil with blood. Elsewhere the sacrifice was to a number of deities, of whom the most important were the Sun God and the God of War; and in some few places, again, no sacrifice whatever was made, the people regarding such practices with horror. The victims, where sacrificed, were in some places of both sexes, in others males only. They might be of any caste or parentage, provided they were not Khonds, for it was contrary to rule to sacrifice a Khond. Foreign children were accordingly purchased and brought up for sacrifice; and they were always kindly treated till they became of age to understand what they were destined for, from which time they were kept guarded and fettered. The *Zanee*, or priest, officiated at the sacrifice, but performed *poojáh* to the idol through the medium of the *Toombá*, a Khond child under seven years of age. For a month prior to the sacrifice there was much feasting and intoxication, with dancing round the Meriáh, or victim, who was adorned with garlands, etc.; and on the day before the rite he was stupefied with toddy and bound at the bottom of a post. The assembled multitude then danced round the post to music, singing hymns of invocation to some such effect as follows:—"O God, we offer a sacrifice to you! Give us good crops in return, good seasons, and health." On the next day the victim was again intoxicated, and anointed with oil, which was wiped from his body by those present, and put on their own heads as a blessing The victim was then carried in procession round the village, preceded by music, and on returning to the post a hog was sacrificed to Zakári Pennu, or the village deity, usually represented by three stones, the blood from the carcass being allowed to flow into a pit prepared to receive it. The victim, made senseless by intoxication, was now thrown into the pit, and his face was pressed down till he died from suffocation in the blood and mire, a deafening noise with instruments being kept up all the time. The Zanee then cut a piece of flesh from the body and buried it with ceremony near the village idol, all the rest of the people present going through the same form after him, while bits of flesh were also interred in the village boundaries. The head and face of the victim were left untouched, and, with the bones when bare, were buried in the pit.

The other crime which was common among the Khonds—namely, the destruction of female children—was justified by them on the score of the difficulty they experienced in getting the children married. The Khonds entertain a low opinion of female morality, and their young men are not eager to take upon themselves the responsibilities of the married state. "How, then," asked the elders, "were the girls under such circumstances to be supported?" Then, again, much vexation was caused to parents by the frequent disruptions of the marriage tie, which necessitated the return of the prices paid for the girls at the time of the marriage; and the best way of obviating such perplexities, it was thought, was to do away with the girls in their infancy. In some places, such as the remoter hills of Chinná Kimedy, male offspring were also killed, but only when the priest or astrologer discovered that the life of the child foreboded evil either to its parents or to the village. In all cases the method of destruction was identical. The infant was placed in a new earthen vessel, the mouth of which was closed, and which was then buried, after being marked with streaks of black and red. Both the Meriáh sacrifice and infanticide have now been tabooed for nearly forty years, and are believed to have been generally abandoned; but all parts of the Khond country have not yet been fully explored, and the news from the wilder corners scarcely come to civilised ears. In some places schools have been set up for the education of Khond children, but it will be a long time yet before these are able to humanise the people to any appreciable extent.

The Saurás.

The Deccan, which includes all the countries to the south of the Nermuddá, was, at one time, the principal seat of the aboriginal tribes—at least, down to the banks of the Godávery. The number of them that burrowed in the caves of its mountains or roamed through its pathless forests was very great, and contributed most to strengthen the Mahrattá and Pindári ranks, in which many of the races were finally absorbed. The remnants that did not disappear in this way still exist; but they are now disjointed and scattered, and, apart from the Gonds, Bheels, and Khonds, and the small migratory tribes of the Central Provinces whom we have noticed, those requiring to be especially mentioned are not many, the most prominent among them being the Saurás, the nearest neighbours of the Khonds to the south, who extend from Chinná Kimedy to the Godávery, or over a region nearly two hundred miles in length, which is almost entirely unexplored. If the Khonds are better looking than the Gonds, the Saurás are, almost to an equal extent, better looking than the Khonds. They are fairer in colour and more athletic in appearance; and their habits too are less dissipated, and their life in general less turbulent. But, when this has been said, everything that can be said in their favour is summed up. They are fiercer than the Khonds, and so entirely destitute of moral sense, that they will unhesitatingly commit the greatest crimes for the paltriest advantages; and even the Khonds are so afraid of them that, though always ready to fight among themselves, they are never anxious to provoke a quarrel with the Saurás. The arms of the two tribes are the same—namely, the battle-axe, and the bow and arrows—and the Saurás are very apt in their use;

but they never attack their enemies except under cover of darkness, not being straightforward in any of their dealings. Even as thieves and plunderers, they always take every unfair advantage of their victims they can, without exercising their courage, though there is no question that they are quite as courageous as any other tribe.

MINOR TRIBES OF THE MADRÁS PRESIDENCY.

For the other races in the Deccan, we have to seek beyond the Godávery. The best part of the Eastern Gháts lies between the Kristná and the Cáuvery rivers, while the Western Gháts, which are higher and of uniform height throughout their entire length, run up from Cape Comorin to the Táptee river, coalescing with the Eastern Gháts between the districts of Coimbatoor and Malábár, where they form together the plateau or nucleus known as the Neilgherry hills. All the wild tribes that still exist in Southern India, exclusive of the Khonds and the Saurás, are crowded in and about this spot; but they are altogether very poor in number, and would scarcely be missed if no mention were made of them.

THE TODÁS.

The upper part of the Neilgherry plateau is inhabited by a wild tribe called the Todás, who are fairer even than the Saurás, from which it has been inferred that they are not aborigines, but came probably as conquerors or immigrants from the sea. They have received much attention mainly from this belief, being too petty in numbers to be noticed on any other account. The subdivisions of the tribe are named: the Peikee, Kenná, Pekkan, Kuttan, and Todi, of which the first is by far the most important. The men are all well-made and above the common height, and have a bold bearing, and open, expressive countenances. Their eyes are large, the nose Roman, and the face always good-humoured. The dress worn by them consists of a short under-garment folded round the waist and fastened to a girdle, and a *chádur*, or mantle, which covers the upper part of the body except the head and the right arm. There is no covering for the head in any weather, and they allow the hair to grow to the length of six or seven inches, parting it from the centre or crown, and wearing it in bushy circlets dangling around. No weapons whatever are carried by them beyond a rod or wand, which helps them in the management of their herds. The women have a modest and retiring demeanour, but are not timid. They have beautiful long tresses, which flow in unrestrained luxuriance over neck and shoulders. Their dress is composed, as that of the men, of an upper and under-garment, but differently worn, the upper garment enveloping the whole frame except the head, which remains uncovered. The ornaments used are necklaces of twisted hair or black thread, with metallic clasps, and, here and there, a knot from which are suspended cowry shells; armlets and bracelets of metal; and a sort of metal chainwork round the waist. Both the men and women are equally dirty; and the hamlets they dwell in, which are called *morts*, and are composed of thatched huts resembling the tilt of a wagon in appearance, are so offensive within that they cannot be entered. The occupation of the race is very peaceful—namely, tending herds of buffaloes only. They do not keep poultry, pigs, sheep, or goats; and even cows are not considered worth bringing up. Their buffaloes are of a much superior breed to those of the low country generally, and the milk they yield is very rich. Their repast is accordingly composed of milk, meal, parched grain, and butter, no luxuries of any sort being cared for; and even the use of salt is unknown to them. The only articles they deal in are butter and *ghee*, which they dispose of in the plains. Their religion is as peaceful as their habits. Their god is represented by a rude stone, to which *ghee* and milk are given, but not blood in any shape. There are priests among them who are bound to lead a life of celibacy, those married before ordination being obliged to live separate from their wives, so that they might divest themselves of all worldly thoughts and wishes, and dedicate their whole time to the contemplation of the Deity. All this represents the race as being inoffensive, virtuous, and happy. But there is another side of the picture to look at. Though endowed with great physical strength and capacity to endure fatigue, they have no agricultural industry to occupy them—no active employment of any kind; and, being indolent and slothful, are not strangers to the passions and vices those habits call forth. The priests in particular lead a very loose life; and cases of plurality of husbands and lovers among the women are frequent.

THE ERILIGÁRU.

Another wild people inhabiting the same plateau are the Eriligáru, who also extend for a short distance into the forests lying at the foot of the hills. They are utterly unskilled in the arts of life, go nearly naked, sleep under trees, and believe themselves to be able to charm tigers. It is said of their women that when they go into the wood in search of food they intrust their children to the tigers, and receive them back, safe and sound, on their return! Their villages are called *cambays*, and are posted on the mountain sides, around a square enclosure in which a large fire is maintained at night to keep them warm and drive away wild beasts from them. They breed goats and cows, catch wild fowls in nets, and tigers in traps, and have large orchards of plantain and lime trees. The language spoken by them is a jargon compounded of the dialects of the different races in their vicinity, by contact with whom they are gradually getting humanised.

THE KÁRUBÁRUS, ETC.

Near the foot of the hills dwell also the Kárubárus, Kurumbárs, and Kohátees, all small, scattered, and harmless races, and the first two of the same character precisely as the Eriligáru—that is, equally unskilled in the arts of life. The occupation these chiefly follow is that of hired labourers to watch the fields against the depredations of birds and wild hogs; but the third, unlike them, are able to cultivate, and also make themselves useful in the hills as smiths, potters, and artisans of every description.

THE SOLIGÁS.

Another wild people, named the Soligás, inhabit the hills in the vicinity of the Cáuvery, and are known as being remarkably rude, and having features not unlike those of the savages of Chittagong, which suggests a possible descent from naval immigrants from across the bay. The huts they build are so wretched that they can hardly live in them, and use them rather as store-rooms and cooking-sheds, sleeping in the open air at night around a fire, with plantain-leaves used both as mattresses and coverings. By day they go nearly naked, but are so busily employed in the depths of the forests that they are rarely seen. They search the forests for lac, beeswax, honey, yams, and esculent leaves; and also hew timber for sale. They keep no domestic animals, nor know the art of killing game; but are not wholly ignorant of agriculture, of which the principal labour devolves on their women. Polygamy is permitted among them, adultery unknown; and the aged are well cared for by their children and relatives.

The Niadis.

The Niadis are another tribe belonging to the same locality. They are very like the Soligás in their habits, living nearly naked, and wandering about in unfrequented places in search of what their woods will yield them. The huts they live in are as miserable as those of the Soligás, and are built under trees, in remote corners. Their principal occupations are to protect the crops from the depredations of wild hogs and birds; to rouse game for hunters; and to catch tortoises and crocodiles, which are eaten with avidity. Marriage, as a ceremony, is unknown among them; but one man lives with one woman only, and infidelity is scarce. Those of them who are shepherds live almost entirely with their flocks, the men sleeping in the open air, wrapping themselves in blankets, while the women and children are sheltered within temporary huts made of blankets, twigs, and leaves. Of their religion all that is known is that they sacrifice to a female spirit yearly.

THE GIPSIES.

The remaining wild tribes of South Deccan may be included under the general head of Gipsies, who are to be seen in every part of India, absorbing all classes of men of the lowest social grades. The race is so well known all over the world, and its counterparts are so like each other in every place, that no lengthened description of it is necessary. As a rule the men are tall, fine-limbed, and bony, but far darker in India than anywhere else; while the women have pretty though sunburnt faces, large, black, and brilliant eyes, and long hair. In some parts of India this people are called Bedyás, in others Náts, in others again Kanjhars and Bájikars, leading the same vagabond life everywhere. Some of them profess Hinduism, others are avowedly Mahomedans; but the main religion of all, the one common bond that binds them together, is thieving, which children weaned from the breast are taught with assiduity. Another common bond between the several septs is a secret language of their own—besides that they ordinarily use—which, it is said, is understood by Gipsies only, and all over the world. Their habits are entirely migratory; but they live in bands, and erect temporary huts wherever they encamp, from which they go about—men and women—as jugglers, strolling players, cattle-gelders, tumblers, and dancing-girls—doing every work in fact except what demands labour and steadiness. Many of the men obtain a living by leading about dancing-bears and monkeys; many more, by catching birds, squirrels, and mungooses; while among the women are those who practise physic, fortune-telling, and tattooing. The men are always as fantastically dressed as they can manage; but the women have frequently nothing beyond a ragged cloth round the waist, which is usually coloured, while the children go naked. In all parts of the world they are represented as eating any kind of food they can come at; and in India they are so uncleanly that they will eat even bullocks and horses that have died of disease. Before marriage there is no constraint on their passions; but after marriage the wife at least is generally faithful. When the parties concerned have agreed to be united the lover proceeds to the hut of his mistress to wed her. Her relations thereupon meet him with a mock refusal, but relent when they find him very pertinacious, and, in giving up the girl, ask him to behave kindly to her. Her forehead is marked by him with *sindoor*, an observance appertaining rather to the country than to the race; and this, completing the ceremony, is followed by a banquet, in which there is as much intoxication as the parties can afford to pay for.

PART II.

THE FRONTIER TRIBES.

CHAPTER I.

TRIBES ON THE NORTH-WESTERN FRONTIER.

IN the preceding pages we have described all the more important internal wild tribes of India, aboriginal or otherwise. It remains now to notice the half-savage frontier tribes, who are for the most part not aborigines of the soil, though they have, from their long residence at the places into which they intruded, become semi-Indianised. On the North-Western frontier the chief of these tribes are: the Beloochees, Páthâns, Wuzeerás, Bunnoochees, Murwátees, Áfreedees, Momunds, and Swátees, all of whom are divided into independent and dependent clans—namely, those occupying the outer face of the frontier, and those occupying its inner side as subjects of the British Government, respectively.

THE BELOOCHEES.

The Beloochees, the southernmost of the races named, are of tall and wiry make, and a rather dark colour, with features decidedly Jewish, but marked by an almost ferocious expression. They are divided into several tribes or clans, of whom the most important are: the Kusránis, Bozdárs, Khutráns, Kosáhs, Singháris, Lisháris, Boogtis, Ghoorchánis, and Madáris, the last two being the most warlike and troublesome. The general character of the entire race is marked by great vindictiveness, treachery, and cruelty, and by a readiness at all times to take offence at the merest trifle; but, on the other hand, they are very hospitable—particularly to the wayfarer and the stranger—free from religious bigotry and fanaticism, and far more truthful when trusted than many of the other races in their neighbourhood. The Khán of Khelát is their nominal sovereign: we say *nominal*, because they are as often found ready to resist as to obey him. They are a mercenary people, who would by nature prefer to act as soldiers, but turn camel-drivers, robbers, and cut-throats as willingly on the price for such service being paid to them. They are passionately fond of field-sports, but are otherwise exceedingly indolent; and they abhor reading and writing as effeminate and contemptible accomplishments. What they are now most famous for is their breed of horses, which, though sorry-looking and insignificant, are well adapted for the life led by their owners, being swift of pace and so inured to labour that they weary out the best racers in pursuit.

The arms of all the tribes are the same—namely, the matchlock, sword, and shield, and their fighting power taken together is not inconsiderable; but they are always at war with each other, and can never heartily combine for any common enterprise. Spirituous liquors are inordinately used by them, and the smoking of *bhang* is incessant, the pipe being in the mouth of both sexes, and at all times. The influence exercised over them by their women is great, it being commonly asserted that, though no confidence can be placed on engagements entered into by the men even when sworn to on the *Korán*, they will never depart from any agreement or stipulation to which their women are parties.

The Páthá*n*s.

The Páthán tribes lying to the north of the Beloochees are of stouter appearance, and, in fact, in physical development count among the finest races of the earth; and the height of pride on the border is to be recognised as a Páthán—that is, of Afghán descent. The race is very warlike, and in times past interfered frequently with the destinies of India; and many of the *kheyls* or tribes make fairly good soldiers to this day—such, for instance, as the Bungaish tribe who inhabit the Kohát district, extending beyond the border into the Khoorum valley. All the men are rough and frank, but neither faithful nor trustworthy; fair to look at, though somewhat bronzed by the hot sun of India; and have no occupation but rapine, which can never be checked except by retaliation and reprisals. They are great fanatics also in religion; and, from one cause or another, have managed to keep their part of the frontier in turmoil at all times.

THE WUZEERÁS.

The Wuzeerás, who come next, hold the Goláree, Bolan, and Soorduk passes, and are a bold and ferocious people, though in soldierly qualities they are very far from being equal to the Pátháns. They are, however, as prone to plunder, and quite as careless of bloodshed, but are held to be comparatively less treacherous, as they will never entrap an enemy by false overtures. They are rather noble specimens of the savage character, and, though wholly without law, are not equally destitute of honour. The principal tribal divisions among them are: the Máhsuds, Áhmedzyes, Othmánzyes, and Bithunnees. The men are all stout and fierce-looking, and the women tall and stately. Their habits are nomadic, and they live usually under tents made of coarse blankets or reed mats, under which old and young huddle together for shelter, careless of the sun or rain. For subsistence they depend mainly on their flocks and herds, and in the winter months they are to be seen yearly moving with their camels, goats, and broad-tailed sheep towards the sheltered plains of Bunnoo. Some of the tribes have also commenced to cultivate. But they are never unready for bolder and more hazardous undertakings, and the discharge of a single matchlock will bring all the clans together to act in concert, either as robbers or soldiers; for, though enemies to all the world, they have no disunion among themselves—which is, in fact, their peculiar trait.

The Bunnoochees.

The Bunnoochees, or inhabitants of Bunnoo, are a mongrel race descended from many races, and differ from each other in stature, complexion, and character. They may nevertheless be generally described as being small in stature and having a shrivelled appearance, along with all the vices of human nature in their worst development. Less cannot be said of them, indeed, than that they bring discredit even on the Afghán name. Their family dissensions are constant on account of their various descent, and it is commonly remarked of them that they are never at peace except when they are at war. They acknowledge no king and hardly a common chief, every *kheyl* having its separate *Mullik*, or master, and being at enmity with all others; but they acknowledge the Ákhoond of Swát as their common high-priest, and are renowned for their fanaticism. Their valley is fertile, and has an abundant supply of water, and the crops grown by them are various, including wheat, rice, sugar-cane, and turmeric. Cattle also are plentiful in it, and the people are necessarily rich in rural wealth of every kind.

THE MURWÁTEES.

The Murwátees are a fine manly race, neighbours of the Bunnoochees, but not like them either in appearance or character. They are a tall and muscular people, frank and simple in their manners, and conspicuous for their generous and manly treatment of their women. Their habits are both agreeable and pastoral, and while some of them are seen cultivating their lands, others are found wandering about with their flocks of goats and laden camels, or occupying temporary huts improvised wherever they encamp. The crops raised by those who cultivate are: wheat, barley, and grain; but their country is sandy, and much distress is felt for want of water, which lies so far below the surface that it is not easy to sink wells to get at it. It has therefore to be procured from distant springs; and a great portion of the time of their women is taken up by this work. Among themselves the people are very factious, their community being divided into two parties which are always quarrelling with each other.

THE ÁFREEDEES.

The Áfreedees have the reputation of being the most formidable of all the Trans-Indus tribes, and hold the principal passes leading into and out of India, along the hills lying between the Kabool river and the Khyber, which form the western boundary of the Peshawar valley. As soldiers they are among the best on the frontier, and every invader of India has had either to take them into his service or to pay for their neutrality. They are fierce by nature and exceedingly unmanageable and untrustworthy, but nevertheless always true to their salt. The main branches of the tribe are: the Ádum, Ooláh, Áká, Meerie, Karum, Bhyrám, and Orukzye *kheyls*, which are always at feud with each other when there is no common enemy to contend with. Their villages are all posted on the loftiest and most rugged hills, which enables them to defy even the hand of power with impunity; and they have accordingly never owned subjection either to the Kabool or to any other Government. In times of peace they are often employed as traders and carriers, and bring salt from the Kohát mines to the Peshawar market; but their innate ferocity inclines them most to deeds of blood. The Áfreedee mother prays that her son may be a successful robber; and the men are so faithless, that they will enter into engagements on the *Korán* after having already made up their minds to break them. They are armed at all times—even when only tilling the ground, or grazing cattle, or driving beasts of burden before them; and will use their weapons on the slightest provocation, or to derive the smallest benefit. The only redeeming virtue in their character is their hospitality. The guest, invited or uninvited, is always welcome and safe; but, once fairly out of his entertainer's door, must protect himself in the best way he can, being no longer entitled to his forbearance.

THE MOMUNDS.

The Momunds are a powerful race, occupying the Peshawar frontier from the left bank of the Kabool river, opposite the Tárturrá Pass, to the right bank of the Swát river in the neighbourhood of Abazie. They live in very small hamlets generally, but have a few large villages and towns; and are divided into several tribes, of whom three are most important —namely, the Tourkzyes, Báeezyes, and Khwáazyes. The tribes best known to the British Government are: the Pindee Áli, Álumzye, and Michnee *kheyls*, whose raids and robberies on the frontier have been incessant. They are all brought up as soldiers, though our more recent knowledge of them in connexion with the just-concluded war in Afghánistán has not altogether established their name for valour. There is no question, however, that they are very audacious as robbers, and, it is said, that they will start up from their devotions, if informed of the approach of a *káfiláh* of merchants, to plunder them, and, after securing their booty, will return to their prayers.

THE SWÁTEES.

The Swátees, the last race to be noticed, consist of various clans united under a loose federal government, with an elective chief, or king, at its head. They do not rank very high as warriors, but are as great plunderers as the rest, and did much outrage in the Peshawar plains in past times, regarding them as their natural hunting-grounds. They never attack any of the warlike races about them, but are savage in dealing with such cultivators, petty traders, and cattle-graziers as they may happen to meet with. Their ways and habits, however, are improving; and they have already begun to cultivate for themselves—namely, cotton, tobacco, and some kinds of pulses on their hills, and rice on their river banks. Their women have a great influence over them; but it is nevertheless said that they are frequently sold, or bartered for money, by their husbands.

All the tribes named above are wild and fierce, and most of them warlike also; and they have all the virtues and vices of the savage state in more or less degree, and often jumbled together in a confused and contradictory manner. Their common religion is Mahomedanism; but the creeds yet more generally understood by them are: "blood for blood" and "fire and sword for infidels." Retaliation and malicious persecution are, in fact, the strongest of all obligations with them; hospitality to all being at the same time an obligation only next in degree. They have no education to speak of, and are superstitious and priest-ridden, their priests and *moolláhs* being as ignorant as themselves. This makes them in some respects dependent on the Hindu *Bunniáhs* living amongst them—the *Bunniáh* on the frontier being something like the Jew as the Jew is, and always has been, all over the world. There is hardly any part even of Central Asia where the *Bunniáh* is not seen. He is insulted and tyrannised over wherever he goes, as the Jew at one time was in Europe; but the trade and mercantile accounts of the whole country he lives in are entirely in his hands, and this reconciles him to the disadvantages of his lot. That lot is very trying at times, for woe to the *Bunniáh* who cannot hide his gold. The only protection against the cupidity of the tribes he lives with is that to be found in the *Zeáruts*, or holy shrines, which are always safe from spoliation, and travellers encamping near which are generally unmolested: and this seems to be a well-observed rule, not only on the north-western frontier, but in all parts of south-western Asia.

CHAPTER II.

TRIBES ON THE NORTHERN FRONTIER.

ON the northern frontier, the Himálayás, though rising almost suddenly in great height, are yet habitable for a considerable distance upland before the snows are reached; but almost all the accessible territory here, from Cashmere downwards, is mainly occupied by different Hindu races, till we come to the borders of Gurhwál and Kumáon.

THE BHOTEES.

The first of the wild tribes to be met with in this place are the Bhotes, or the Bhotees, a cross-breed probably between the Khásiáhs and the Huniás, who occupy the passes and even the centres and crests of the mountains between Busehár and Kumáon. Their appearance, manners, and peculiarities are very like those of the Khásiáhs, whom we shall presently describe, while their dialect is the same with that of Thibet. The habits of the race are nomadic, and they dwell chiefly in tents, almost entirely monopolising the trade across the mountains, which is carried, for the most part, on the back of their sheep. They also cultivate a little, principally in the Terái, where they always lodge during the winter months for *dhoopseknâ*, as they call it—that is, to bask in the sun—and where they graze their herds on the rich herbage with which they are overgrown.

The Khásiáhs.

The Khásiáhs are the immediate neighbours of the Bhotees, inhabiting the districts of Gurhwál and Kumáon, or all the mountain tract lying between the Alakánanda and the Káligungá. The race is an ancient one, enumerated in the *Institutes* of Menu under the name of Khásas, among the several Kshetriya races referred to by the legislator. They still claim to be of Rájpoot descent; but even that would not make them aborigines of the country, the Rájpoots themselves being nothing more than Scythians. As now seen they exhibit clearly a mixture of Mongolian and Indian blood, though they have adopted the language and customs of the Hindus, and are anxious to be counted with them. They are strong in numbers, for they form about nine-tenths of the population of the provinces they inhabit, and extend from the foot of the mountains to the Terái, which separates them from Rohilkund. The men are of middle size, dark and meagre in appearance, but well framed and active, and of loftier stature than the Bhotees and other mountaineers in their neighbourhood. Their women have handsome features, though they look sunburnt and toil-worn. The dwelling of the race is chiefly under tents, and the ordinary garment of the men is a long black blanket, which is indispensable to them. The dress of the women is a coarse cloth worn round the waist, with the black blanket in addition passed over the head and shoulders. The character of the people being peaceable, no arms are carried by them except sticks to drive away wild animals. The women wear ornaments in the shape of metal anklets and bracelets, and weighty rings in their ears and noses. Polyandry prevails very widely among them, and very frequently a family of brothers has only one wife in common. Chastity and conjugal affection hardly exist; but their attachment for children is very strong. They are also sober and good-humoured, and the women are very patient under privations. The men being excessively indolent, the entire labour of domestic economy and agriculture is left to the women, with the exception of ploughing and harrowing, which is performed by the men. It speaks much to the credit of the women therefore, that, in every part of their country where the declivity of their hills will admit of the operations of a plough or spade, small plots of ground are to be seen, all in a high state of cultivation, and many of them ranged in little terraces one above another, supported by walls of loose stone. One portion of the race—namely, those who do not live at any great distance from the plains—migrate annually to the upper part of the Terái during the cold weather, to "bask in the sun" like the Bhotees, taking their cattle with them to graze. They are always accompanied by their families, and employ themselves in cultivating the best and driest spots of the forest with barley and wheat, which they reap and carry back with them, returning again to gather their later crops, should they have sown any. These opportunities are also taken to dispose of their *ghee*, honey, and the produce of their hills generally, in exchange for such luxuries as are only to be obtained from the plains. They are so honest that property amongst them is always left exposed even when the owners are absent from home, the use of lock and key being unknown. The only precaution taken on such occasions is to fence their grounds carefully with a view to keep out wild animals from them.

THE BOKSÁS.

In the forests at the foot of the Sewálik hills live the Boksás, who are as spare in habit as the Khásiáhs, but shorter in stature, and are distinguished by broad faces, depressed noses, thick lips, and very scanty hair on the face. They are quite as simple and inoffensive as the Khásiáhs, but, if possible, yet more ignorant and unthrifty, and so very indolent that they object to all labour which is not absolutely necessary for subsistence. They have no arts or manufactures among them; and the little clothing they wear is imported. They cultivate to some extent, but the produce is never abundant enough to supply their wants fully. Their food is very simple, consisting ordinarily of bread made of wheat, barley, or millet, or of rice and *dál*, seasoned with wild herbs cooked as greens; but their laziness is so great that they are often, for want of these even, compelled to subsist on yams and berries only. Flesh in any quantity they cannot obtain, for, though fond of deer and wild pigs, they will not take the trouble to hunt for them, nor will they breed any domestic animals, even fowls being but rarely reared by them. The chief products of their forests are bamboos and timber, which are cut for export. They also collect drugs and gums for sale, and wash for gold in the Soná Nadi and the Rámgungá, getting in exchange for what they collect tobacco and spirits, of both of which they are equally fond. Their women, however, are not ordinarily allowed to get drunk with them, for "what need have they for spirits," say the men, "when they have neither to go out into the jungles, nor to sit up whole nights on a *máchán* watching crops?" One division of the race lives to the east of the Rámgungá, where it is concentrated, while the other dwells on the west of the river, and is more loosely scattered. The Eastern Boksás show an invincible dislike to settle down on any particular spot for more than two years, though they never migrate outside of their forests or the Terái ; but the Western are not so restless, and many of them will never shift from their villages at all. There are some Boksá villages also in the Deyrá Dhoon, where the people are called Mehrás, though acknowledged by the other Boksás to be of the same caste with themselves. They all conform to the Hindu religion, though in an ignorant and unmeaning way, and in all small matters generally adhere to Hindu customs, as they understand them. The moral character of the race is excellent, and their good humour can only be compared with that of the Khásiáhs.

THE THÁROOS.

Side by side with the Boksás live the Thároos, who occupy all the Terái from eastern Rohilkund, along the frontiers of Oude, to Goruckpore and the Gunduck. The great mass of them are now subjects of the Nepál Government, having been transferred to it with the Oude Terái. They are very similar to the Boksás in several respects, but neither will acknowledge any relationship or connexion with the other. Both are apparently of Mongolian extraction, but seem to have intermixed largely with the Indian races, some of whom, such as the Koles, they resemble to a considerable extent. The Thároos are very shy and timid, but very frank and truthful, and their women have a name for chastity. They live in grass huts, and are less migratory than the eastern Boksás, more nearly resembling the western tribe in that respect. Their principal occupation is cultivation, and their tillage is peculiar in this, that it leaves large wastes between the patches that are cultivated. Unlike the Boksás, they always raise food-grains enough for their use, their women, who are hardy, assisting them greatly in husbandry. They are expert huntsmen also, and eat the game they kill, as well as other flesh, not excluding that of animals that have died of disease; and they drink quite as largely as the Boksás, the habit having perhaps been equally forced on both by their residence in the Terái.

The Limboos.

The Limboos are found on the Nepál frontier, and between Nepál and Sikkim, and form a numerous tribe, which is said to have come originally from the province of Chung in Thibet. They are scarcely ever seen beyond the Teestá except as strangers; but many of them have come and settled in and about Darjeeling. Like the other hill-tribes near them, they are short in stature, fair in complexion, and completely beardless; but they are less fleshy than some of them, as, for instance, the Lepchás.

The physical differences between the several races here located are, in fact, slender, and not obvious to strangers, and hence the usual practice of grouping them together. In former times, the Limboos were a warlike race; but they are now almost wholly given to agriculture, cattle-grazing, and petty trading. The two most important septs among them are named Hung and Rái. The habits and customs are the same with both, their dress consisting of wide trousers and a jacket, and their principal weapon being the *kookri.* They live in huts, which are very rudely made and inconvenient, a whole family having rarely more than one apartment. In religion they affect the Hinduism of Nepál, but in reality have gods and goddesses of their own, and one Supreme Deity over all. They do not build temples to any of these, nor make images of them; and their worship consists simply of offerings and sacrifices.

THE MURMIS.

The Murmis are also of Thibetan origin, and are found in all parts of the Nepál mountains, and in the Sikkim country, as far to the east as the Teestá. They are a numerous tribe in their original country, and as seen on the frontier are less changed in their habits than other races of similar descent. They are strongly made and active, and taller than the Limboos; but, though good-tempered, are not held to be of an equally cheerful disposition. Their habits are pastoral and agricultural, with this especial peculiarity in them, that they feed their sheep and goats on the highest elevations near the snows, and cultivate as great heights as are capable of producing maize and *murwá*. Their villages are accordingly perched on sites from 4000 to 6000 feet high, where they live in cottages built of stone and thatched with grass. Their religion is the Buddhism of Thibet. They are said to be very kind to strangers.

THE VÁYUS.

The Váyus, or Háyus, are another race dwelling on the confines of Nepál, on or about the tract where the Koosi enters India. They have a tradition among them of having at one time been a powerful people, but, as seen at present, are a very small race, verging gradually to extinction. Physically, they are of a medium height, brown colour, hazel eyes, and long black hair; and in character are at the same time inoffensive and industrious. They are employed chiefly in cultivation, and also in collecting the produce of their mountains.

THE KERÁNTIS.

A more powerful people in their neighbourhood are the Kerántis, who are said at one time to have held dominion down to the delta of the Ganges.

They are tall in stature and well-made, having a pale brown colour, well-formed face, large oval eyes, and straight jet-black hair. They are mostly subjects of Nepál, and in their own hills bear a fierce and quarrelsome character; but have a better name in Darjeeling, where they are much valued as servants, both menial and military service being now sought for by them to some extent. Their principal occupation on the hills is cultivation; and they raise crops of maize, buckwheat, millet, peas, rice, and cotton. They have no craftsmen among them, and are necessarily compelled to buy the implements, utensils, and ornaments they use. Their houses are built on hill slopes, being raised on the outer side on wooden posts to give them a level. The walls are of thick reeds plastered, and the roof of grass. Each family builds separately for itself, and children separate from their parents the moment they get married. The occupations of the women are spinning and weaving cotton of native growth, and thus all the clothes they wear are home-made. They also make the liquors—fermented and distilled—which they drink. Their usual way of obtaining a wife is either to buy her, or to earn her by labour in her father's family. Divorce can be had at the pleasure of either party; but, if the wife seek it, her family has to refund the price that was paid for her. Great veneration is paid by this people to their dead, whom they bury on the hill tops. They have no clear idea of religion, but two great religious festivals are held by them annually, one being in honour of Khyimmo, or the household deity, and the other in honour of the Sámkhá, or souls of the dead.

The Lepchás.

The Lepchás inhabit the southern face of the Himálayás, from the Tambár branch of the Koosi on the west, to the mountains of Bootán on the east, and are the subjects respectively of Nepál, Sikkim, and Bootán. They have been spoken of as the aborigines of the mountain forests surrounding Darjeeling; but there is less doubt that they are of Mongolian descent. The primary divisions of the race are two, named Rong and Khambá, of whom the former only profess to be indigenous, while the latter assert that they came originally from Khám, a province of China. They are both precisely alike in appearance, being short in size, but bulky for their height, and rather fleshy than sinewy. Their faces are broad and flat, nose depressed, eyes oblique; they have no beard at all, and a very little only of moustache. The complexion is olive, and may be called fair, and the children have even a ruddy tinge, which, however, is lost in adolescence. The total absence of beard, and the fashion of parting the hair along the crown of the head, gives the males an effeminate appearance, and, the robes of the two sexes being fashioned nearly alike, it is not always easy to distinguish them. The dress of the men consists of a cotton cloak, with a loose jacket also for those who can afford to have two, both bound round the waist; while the women have first a petticoat of cotton cloth, and over it something like a loose bedgown, fastened by a girdle. The hair is worn in long plaits by both sexes; but, while the men have a single pigtail, the women have two. The ornaments in use consist of necklaces of coloured beads and corals, and earrings; the women having, of course, more of both than the men. The arms of the men are the *kookri* and a long knife called *bán*, which they use nimbly in all work; besides which they have a bamboo bow and iron-pointed arrows. But they are not warriors, and use their weapons only against wild beasts and for cutting down forests; and they have their spade and hoe to help them in agriculture. They are not good cultivators, however, and, having no ploughs, only scrape the ground to put in the seeds, which does not yield them more food-grains than they require. The crops raised are: rice, wheat, barley, and millet; and, when the supply of these is very inadequate, they are obliged to subsist upon ferns, bamboo roots, and the innumerable succulent plants to be found in their mountains, besides which they eat all kinds of flesh, including beef and pork. Tea is a favourite beverage with them, and is brought from China; but they are even more fond of fermented and spirituous liquors, without however being given to excess. They make their beer themselves, and it is said to be refreshing; but the art of distillation is not known to them. In habits they are very dirty, and also excessively indolent, and, preferring to spend their time in hunting and loitering, they leave all out and indoor work to their women. They are perpetually moving about, and never remain in one place for more than three years, which is the period usually allowed by all nomad tribes for the freshness of the virgin soil to get exhausted. They have necessarily no permanent villages; but the huts they set up are, nevertheless, well made, being constructed entirely of bamboos, and thatched with the same material split up. Their cheerfulness of disposition is proverbial, and they are also honest—so much so, that theft is uncommon among them. Their good nature, too, is great, and though constantly wrestling and jumping, they are never seen to fight or quarrel with one another. In religion they are Buddhists, and are said to be somewhat superior to their neighbours, the Booteáhs, in morality. Chastity in adult girls previous to marriage is neither to be met with nor cared for; and the marriages are often allowed to take place on credit—that is, breakable if the payment bargained for is not made within the specified time; but girls married are usually faithful to their husbands.

THE BOOTEÁHS.

The Booteáhs are the inhabitants of Bootán, where they are independent; but they also occupy the alpine regions adjacent to the British frontier, which are known by the name of the Doárs, and are now subject to the British Government. They can hardly be counted among the *wild* tribes of India, for they are, for the most part, in good circumstances, and have a certain amount of civilisation among them; though there is no doubt that, in some particular respects, they are in worse plight even than the worst savages we have described. The best account we have of them is that given by Sir Ashley Eden, who went to their country as an envoy in 1864. The mission was unsuccessful, and led to the Bootán war, by which the Doárs were acquired; but since then the British frontier has been better respected than it ever was before.

The Booteáhs are a short, square-built people, with the true Kálmuck countenance—that is, having a broad flat face, small and oblique eyes, a low and short nose, and a large mouth, all shown to the best advantage by a good-humoured expression, which imparts attraction even to their physical defects. The men are, for the most part, stout and ruddy, and the women healthy-looking, if not handsome; but they are both so excessively dirty that it is never convenient to admire them except at a distance. Their dress is the ordinary Tartar dress, consisting of large boots with trousers stuffed into them, caftans girded round the waist, and little bonnets edged with black sheep's skin; the dress of the women varying to this extent, that they substitute a long cloak with loose sleeves for the coat worn by the men. Neither men nor women are much fond of indulging in ablutions, and their garments are never changed till they rot off; nor does it add to their attractions that the front of their coats is used as a pouch for holding everything, cooked rations included. Of one sect, the Dharmias, it is said that they never wash even their hands and faces except on particular occasions of religious ceremony, and use the skirts of their dress to cleanse alike their persons and cooking utensils. The ornaments most in fashion with all are large pins and amber beads; and corals are also worn by those who can afford to have them. The coarser clothes worn are woven by themselves, but the finer fabrics, whether of wool or silk, are imported from China and Thibet; and even a great portion of the food they live upon has to be procured from other places, as they are neither good agriculturalists nor good animal-breeders. The crops they raise are excessively scanty; and, though sheep and goats form the principal means of transport in their country, they have to be obtained from villages beyond the southern base of their mountains. Trade is therefore an object of great importance to them, and they hold in their hands a complete monopoly of the carrying trade with Thibet. The articles supplied to them from India are: grain of various kinds, sugar, spices, tobacco, cotton cloths, and hardware; while their imports to India consist of shawl wool, woollen cloths, *chowries*, or tails of the yak or mountain ox, and ponies. It is from this, their principal occupation, that the modicum of civilisation they can boast of has been derived; and many Booteáhs are able to read and write. Their houses, also, are well built, and made of good materials, though they are better looking from without than convenient to live in. They make, too, the paper they write upon, and have acquired knowledge of distillation, which enables them to manufacture the spirits they drink. But against these advances, so far as they are such, has to be noted their extreme laxity in morals, which it is not possible to exceed. The marriage tie is so loose that chastity is quite unknown amongst them. The husbands are indifferent to the honour of their wives, and the wives do not care to preserve that which has no value attached to it. Polyandry prevails among them—largely in some parts of the country, less so in others—but even the very slight restriction implied by the institution is not observed. The intercourse of the sexes is, in fact, promiscuous; and the law of inheritance in Bootán has reflectively laid down that, on the death of a Booteáh, his property is to go to the Deb or Dhurm Rájáh, and not to the children, it being impossible to determine whose children they are. The religion followed is greatly influenced by the peculiar situation and pursuits of the people. In Bootán itself they are all followers of Buddha, or the Llámá; but those inhabiting the Doárs have for a long time accepted many Hindu prejudices and superstitions.

The Meches.

The Meches inhabit the forest portion of the Nepál Terái, and are neighbours on the hill side of the Booteáhs, Lepchás, and Limboos, and on the plain side of the Koches and the Dhimáls, of whom the latter are now nearly extinct. They are nomads of Mongolian descent, and resemble the Booteáhs in form, features, and language; and their position on the frontier has always been that of slaves to the Booteáhs. Being quiet and inoffensive, they have accepted this condition with meekness; but they have taken advantage of their migratory habits gradually to spread further to the south beyond Booteáh influence, and now occupy a large portion of Central and Lower Assam. They hold small estates direct from the Government, and cultivate them principally with cotton, just in the same fashion as the Lepchás, but paying greater attention to their tillage. They are very good-tempered and cheerful, and so inured to labour that no amount of work ever makes them unhappy. At present they are noted for their weakness; but they have tales among them which speak of the achievements of their fathers with the bow and arrows among the wild beasts. For trade they have no aptness, and military service they eschew; but they are not constitutionally apathetic, and are very healthy to look at. The air of the Terái, which is so hurtful to others, suits them best; and they have never attempted to get into higher ranges, the climate of which, they say, does not agree with them. Their habits and manners are modified according to the neighbourhood they live in. In the upper parts of the Terái they eat everything; but they do not eat cows, buffaloes, and fowls within the pale of Hindu influence. Alongside of the Assamese they copy the Assam habits faithfully, and chew *pán* and opium and smoke tobacco to excess, drinking spirits also, though not inordinately. The actual state of society among them is still rather primitive. The men and women share equally in the labours of the field, but beyond weaving, which is practised by the women, they do not know much of the industrial arts. They have commenced to learn these, nevertheless, wherever they have come in contact with the Hindus, and there is little doubt that they will finally be absorbed among them. Their women are decidedly prepossessing, and have a fine complexion and expressive eyes; and daughters are much prized by their parents because they are a source of wealth to them, as a wife has always to be purchased. The female dress is the Bengali *sáree*, but made generally of red silk. The unmarried youths of both sexes have sleeping quarters distinct from their family residences, each at one end of their village, so that they are kept as widely asunder as possible. But they nevertheless manage to get together to make love, and marriage with them always takes the form of forcible abduction, after which the bride is retained by her ravisher for some days. An arrangement is then come to between him and her parents, by which the latter recognise the union on the price of their daughter being paid to them. Polygamy is unknown, and infidelity uncommon; while prostitution takes the form of *niká* marriages, by which all widows are disposed of. The religion professed by the race is the Sivite form of Hinduism; but their manners and customs are their own and have nothing in common with it, as is exemplified, for instance, by the *niká* marriage custom referred to, which is a Mahomedan and not a Hindu institution. They have, also, neither castes nor Bráhmans among them; and, what is more, they sacrifice pigs and fowls at the shrine of Káli and to their household and river gods, which the most unorthodox Hindu could never venture to imitate. They are, in fact, passing through a transition state now, verging decidedly towards Hinduism, though still remaining at a great distance from it.

THE KOCHES.

The Koch race of northern Bengal were very powerful before the Mahomedan conquest of India, and even now are semi-independent, and have a rájáh, or ruler, of their own. Their present nucleus is Cooch Behár, but stragglers from their body are to be met with in several parts of Assam, and in all the country from Rungpore to the hills. The primitive or Páni Koches lived amid the woods, but there are few of them now to be met with. Where still existing they claim to be of the same race with the Gáros, and the language and customs of the two peoples certainly do agree to a great extent. The intermarriage of the other Koch tribes with the Hindus has very considerably civilised them, so much so that their original character can hardly be distinguished at present with certainty. They resemble the Bengalis now more than any other people, except that they breed hogs and poultry and eat them, and make a fermented liquor to drink, which Bengalis of the higher classes do not. The cultivation among the Koches is mainly with the hoe; but they weed their crops, which is not usual with the cognate races around them. Their clothing is made by their women, and is generally coloured blue bordered with red, the material being cotton of their own growth; and they are certainly better clothed than the mass of Hindus around them.

Their huts are also well made, though not raised on posts like the houses of the Indo-Chinese races generally. The only arms they carry are spears; but they are scarcely ever used even against wild beasts. Their devotion to the sex is peculiar: they leave to women all the cares of property, and the women in return are most industrious in weaving, spinning, brewing, planting, and sowing: in a word, in doing everything not above their strength. When a woman dies the property is divided among her daughters; and when a man marries he goes to live with his wife's mother, and obeys her as dutifully as his wife does. Re-marriage of widows is allowed; and widows left with property can always get young men for their second and subsequent husbands. The mass of the race have long become Mahomedans, and our description here has reference only to the small remnant of it that still bears the old tribal name. One clan of the tribe, the Rájbunsis, worship Hindu deities and have adopted Hindu manners, and the Rájáh of Cooch Behár belongs to it. He has been to England, and has married the daughter of a Bengali gentleman, Mr. Keshub Chunder Sen, the Bráhmo Apostle, and a thorough reorganisation of the race may fairly be expected from him.

CHAPTER III.

TRIBES ON THE NORTH-EASTERN FRONTIER.

FROM the east of Bootán to the farthest extremity of Assam the Himálayas are occupied by a great variety of wild tribes, with all of whom the British Government has not yet come into contact. The surface of the country is almost uniformly represented by a confused medley of mountains and narrow valleys, watered by innumerable hill-streams, and the authority of the Government over it is so indefinite that the exterior frontier line has not even been attempted to be laid down. In general the mountains are clothed with magnificent forests infested by savage inhabitants, and all that has been secured to the present time is a very superficial dominion over those of them that live at the base of the outer hills, who receive stipends from the Government in various shapes for such submission or forbearance as they have agreed to. Their title to black-mail was an old privilege enjoyed by them under the native Governments of Assam, which the British Government, on coming to the possession of that country, was obliged to commute into the annual money payments now made, as the raiding propensities of the tribes could not otherwise be controlled. The chief of these peoples are: the Ákhás, Duflás, Meeris, Mishmees, and Ábors, who occupy the upper valley of the Brahmapootra, while, *vis-à-vis* to them, the southern valley is inhabited by the Khámptis, Singphos, and Nágás, who divide the British and Burman dominions from each other. To the west of the Nágás are the Cossyáhs and Gáros, and also the Cácharese, Meckirs, and Kookies, the latter running south by the Hylákándy valley to the frontier of Chittagong. All these tribes are yet exceedingly wild, and it will take many years of direct interference with them to improve their condition. On the south of the Brahmapootra the policy of permanent occupation and direct management has already been inaugurated in the Nágá, Gáro, Cossyáh and Jynteáh, and Chittagong Hill-tracts, as annexation there does not involve any indefinite extension of responsibility; but the difficulty on the northern side is that the same course cannot be there followed without trenching unduly on the independent States of Thibet and Bootán.

THE ÁKHÁS.

The Ákhás come immediately after the Booteáhs, and have the characteristics of a Mongolian descent prominently developed in a broad round face, flat nose, and small eyes. They are not a very numerous people; but have the credit of being extremely savage, and used at one time to be much feared for their daring raids, especially by their nearest neighbours, the inhabitants of Chárdwár. They are divided into two primary clans—namely, the Házári-Kháwá Ákhás, or "hearth eaters," and the Káppáchore Ákhás or "cotton stealers," both of whom were great outlaws, and defied the power of the zemindárs with impunity. This led to an expedition being undertaken against them in 1836, and to the conclusion of an arrangement by which their good conduct was secured by the payment of pensions to their chiefs: and the oaths then taken have hitherto been generally respected. They are so uncivilised that they do not know how to cultivate; but they tend flocks and herds, and live on them, eating the flesh of cows without touching the milk, which they abominate. Their arms are: the spear, bow and arrows, and a sharp sword, or *dáo*, which is used for all purposes. Of religion their idea is very indistinct; but they fear their mountains and torrents, and the dense jungles in which their cattle go astray. The dead are buried by them, and the spirits of their deceased ancestors are venerated.

THE DUFLÁS.

The Duflás are the nearest neighbours of the Ákhás to the east, and are believed to belong to the same family, both being again held to be nearly akin to the Hill Meeris. They are shorter in stature than both the Ákhás and the Meeris, and inferior to them in *physique;* but their habits and manners are in several respects identical with those of the other tribes. The subdivision into clans among them is very great, and it is still believed by many that they are not so much a single tribe as a collection of numerous cognate clans almost incapable of combining with each other. They are nevertheless always much feared as plunderers, and at one time it was found necessary to establish a line of military posts along the frontier to prevent their raids. The operations of 1836, which were directed against them as much as against the Ákhás, led to the same successful results in both cases. Their good conduct was secured by money payments, and since then they have very successfully cultivated the plains they harried. They are rich also in flocks and herds now, even more than the Ákhás; but here their superiority over them ceases. Polygamy exists among both tribes; but polyandry is far more common among the Duflás, and chastity almost unknown.

THE MEERIS.

Beyond the Duflás are found, in the lower ranges, the Meeris, and, in the upper ranges, the Ábors, to whom the Meeris owed a kind of fealty in former days. The assertion of British authority in Assam relieved the Meeris from this thraldom, and they took advantage of it to remove themselves beyond the pale of Ábor influence to the quarters they now occupy. The Ábors made many applications to the Government authorities to send back to them their runaway slaves, and the lack of any response was one main cause of the unfriendly bearing they subsequently exhibited. The Meeris are believed to be of the same stock with the Ábors, and are tall, powerful men, with the Mongolian features strikingly developed. Their usual head-dress is a cap of cane or bamboo work, covered with tiger or leopard skin, including the tail, which hangs down the back. The nether garment is the *kopni*, which is passed between the legs and fastened to a girdle of canework, while the upper robe is a cloth wrapped round the body and pinned so as to resemble a coat. The women wear a small petticoat made of filaments of cane woven together; and this is often their only garment. The Hill Meeris are rudely armed with *dáos*, and bows and arrows, the last tipped with a deadly vegetable poison; but the Meeris of the plains have always followed peaceful occupations mainly, and go unarmed; and, since they have been relieved of their dependence on the Ábors, have become very prosperous traders and cultivators, the women sharing in field labours with the men. The grounds set apart for cultivation by them are always divided into patches, of which about one-fifth are cultivated at a time, each patch for two years, and every patch in its turn. Fresh ground is never broken so long as the available fallow is found to be sufficient. The crops raised are: *dous* rice, millet, maize, yams, sweet potatoes, tobacco, and red pepper. They also breed pigs and cattle, and rear poultry, and, having no caste prejudices, eat them, though from their intercourse with the Assamese they try to imitate them in most other respects. It is said that they eat even the flesh of tigers; but they do not allow their women to share this food with them, lest it should make them too strong-minded for control! Combining for mutual support, they live in communities, under hereditary chiefs, and occasionally one chief is acknowledged as the highest over a cluster of communities. Their houses are well-made, and have raised floors, with space underneath for their pigs and poultry. One long apartment in each building is used by the whole family to eat, drink, and sleep in, while other portions of it are partitioned off for various domestic purposes; but the fear of the Ábors is still so great that the family valuables are invariably kept buried. Their granaries, on the contrary, are always kept unprotected in the midst of their fields, the villagers having perfect confidence in each other's good faith and honesty. Polygamy is practised among them, especially by the chiefs; and, after the death of a chief, his son becomes the husband of all his widows, except of the mother who bore him. Instances of polyandry are also known. All the girls, in fact, have their prices, the largest price for the best-looking girl varying from twenty to thirty pigs, and, if one man cannot give so many, he has no objection to take partners to make up the number.

THE ÁBORS.

The Ábors lie to the north of the Meeris up to the borders of Thibet, and are a blunt, independent, and warlike people, much feared by all their neighbours. They call themselves *Pádam*, the name *Ábor*—"rude or barbarous"—having been given to them by the Assamese. Apparently they are of the same race with the Meeris and the Duflás, or, at all events, there is no very material difference between them. The distinct sects and settlements of the Ábors are many, the most important of them being the Bor, Membu, Silook, Sissee, Pádoo, Páshee, and Bomjeer tribes respectively. In general terms, they are regarded as confederate states; but each community is governed by its own laws, devised and administered on purely democratic principles. The laws are made by the people collected together, every individual having an equal vote. No chief is expressly acknowledged; but there are always a few persons in every community who, either from superior wealth, hereditary distinction, or real ability, exert strong influence over the rest, swaying them almost as they list. Membu is the largest of the settlements known, but those occupying the loftier ranges behind are believed to be of greater consequence, especially the Bor Ábors, who seem to be the most powerful. The contact of the British Government with the Ábors is of comparatively recent date. The first expedition against them was sent up in 1859, and another was got ready in 1861, when overtures were received for a peaceful arrangement of differences. Several communities came in, and, in consideration of the democratic nature of their unions, payment in kind to the communities was agreed to instead of money payments to the chiefs, a change which gave to each individual an interest in keeping the peace.

The appearance of the Ábors is not very prepossessing. They are nearly as tall as the Meeris, but are clumsy-looking and sluggish. Their features are Mongolian; and they have deep sepulchral voices. The women resemble the Chinese to some extent in features and complexion, but are of a coarser type, and many of them are disfigured with *goître*. The dress of the men consists of a *dhoti* made of the bark of the *uddál* tree, which also serves the purposes of a carpet to sit upon and of a covering. It is tied round the loins, and hangs down behind in loose strips like a white bushy beard, and is used too as a pillow at night by being rolled up. The rest of his equipment depends entirely on the taste of each individual. Some wear plain basket caps; others have cane caps covered with skins; others, again, use caps of helmet fashion. Almost every man has a woollen coat, while those who have not are dressed in skins; and necklaces of blue beads are worn as ornaments. The female dress is a piece of cloth suspended by a string round the loins, and reaching to the knees, while another piece is folded round the bosom, though this latter is often dispensed with in hot weather, the exposure of the person above the waist not being considered indelicate. The decorations worn by both men and women are strings of beads, which, in the case of the latter, reach from the neck to the waist; and enormous earrings of nearly an inch in diameter, to make place for which the lobes of the ear are gradually distended and enlarged from childhood. The women add to these anklets of cane tightly laced, so as to set off the fine swell of their legs, the canes being sometimes tinged with a light-blue colour to heighten the effect; and a row of embossed plates of bell metal is worn as an undergarment, suspended from the loins—but by young females only, till they become mothers. The hair of both sexes is cropped close, by lifting it up on a knife and chopping it all round with a stick; and both men and women are tattooed, many bearing the mark of the cross on the forehead, though not as an emblem of salvation, notwithstanding the assumption of some observers that the earlier fathers of the Church who operated in India might perhaps have converted their ancestors! The arms of the warriors are spears, long straight swords, daggers, and crossbows and arrows, the last used with or without poison; and their caps and helmets are ornamented with the hair of the yak dyed red, boar's tusks, and the beak of the bucceros. The salute of an Ábor chief is usually a shrill whoop, not unlike the crowing of a cock; and in their meetings in council this cry is every now and then renewed, while the right foot is made to break the ground constantly—like that of a pawing steed.

In disposition the Ábors are said to be like tigers—so much so, that they cannot live alongside of each other in peace. Their houses are accordingly scattered, singly or in groups of two or three at most, all over the mountainous country they inhabit. The huts are, as a rule, well made and convenient, though not very roomy. Their cultivation is almost all in the plains, and consists of rice, cotton, tobacco, maize, ginger, red pepper, a great variety of esculent roots and pumpkins, and the sugar cane. To these they have added opium, the use of which is increasing. They do not break new lands unnecessarily. When the land they were cultivating gets exhausted, they revert to that which was lying fallow, whereby the whole space from their village to the most distant point of their cultivation gets cleared and appropriated while the rest of the forest is spared. The boundaries of each man's clearing are denoted by upright stones, and property in cultivated or fallow land is recognised and respected. Their implements of husbandry are long knives and swords, crooked bamboos to scrape the earth with, and pointed sticks to make holes, into which they dexterously shoot the seed grains to be sown. In all agricultural labours the men are assisted by their wives; but the entire work does not devolve on the women, as among some other tribes. They also know the art of working iron, and make their own *dáos* and bells, some of which they export. The most common occupation of all, however, is hunting; and they eat the flesh of every animal they kill, including that of the elephant, the rhinoceros, and the buffalo, but express an abhorrence of beef. They drink a fermented liquor prepared by themselves, but have a marked partiality for brandy if they can get it, and are rather intemperate drinkers. The women among them are well treated, though hardworked; and polygamy, if permitted, is not usually practised. This, however, seems peculiar to the Pádoo community especially. Among the Sissee Ábors a man has often as many wives as he can afford to buy. Polyandry is also practised; and a common rule with the Sissees is for two or three brothers to have a number of wives in common. Marriages are ostensibly arranged by parents ; but, in point of fact, the young people concerned always settle the affair between themselves—seldom marrying, however, out of their own clan. A feast is the only ceremony observed, besides which the lover has to find such exquisite delicacies as field mice and squirrels for his mistress and her parents. In demeanour the women are equally free from timidity and levity; but they are at the same time totally devoid of modesty, and chastity is not an Ábor virtue. Of their religion all that is certainly known is that they sacrifice to a great number of deities supposed to reside in their woods and mountains, and believe in a future state of rewards and punishments. They have no medicine for the sick: for every disease there is a spirit who has to be mollified. The sacrifices are necessarily constant ; and every sacrifice furnishes an excuse for a debauch.

THE MISHMEES.

The hills which close the north-east corner of Assam are occupied by the Mishmees, a short sturdy race, of fair complexion and great activity, whose features betray a cross between the Mongolian and the Hindu. Though extremely wild-looking, they are comparatively inoffensive; but they are exceedingly dirty, and almost equally dishonest.

They are divided into a vast number of petty clans, of whom the Choolkáttá, the Táen, and the Myjoo are the most important. The Choolkáttás, or "crop-haired," are the most western, and occupy the mountains on the banks of the Dibong; and they are also reputed to be the most savage. The Táens extend eastward from the Choolkáttás, and the Myjoos eastward after them, being the most remote. The warlike clans are the Choolkáttás and the Myjoos, while the Táens and several smaller tribes, called the Mároos, Manneáhs, Tshees, Dháhs, Mlees, etc., have always been decidedly peaceful. They are altogether a numerous people, but exceedingly indigent, and ill-provided both with food and clothing. Agriculture is carried on by them in the most rude and simple manner, and their supply of food-grains is necessarily scanty. They are richer in flocks and herds, and are so dependent on animal food for subsistence that no animal, from an elephant to a mouse, comes amiss to them. The dress of all classes is very inferior, and that of the lower orders scarcely decent; but the chiefs wrap themselves in comfortable long cloaks of Thibet wool, besides wearing an apology for a *dhoti* round the loins. The female dress is more copious, consisting of a coloured *sáree* wrapped round the waist and a rather scanty bodice sometimes covered with a thicker garment. Both men and women wear the hair long, and have it turned up into a knot on the crown of the head; but the

Choolkáttás crop the hair in front, which makes them hideous to look at. The head-dress of all tribes is either a fur cap or a wicker helmet; and the weapons usually carried are a spear or a cross-bow, and a large heavy knife, which helps them to open out passages through their jungles. By far the most remarkable article of their equipment, however, is the earring, which is quite as massive as that worn by the Ábors. They also carry a pouch of monkey's skin at the girdle, to carry tobacco and a case of flint and stone, and have always a pipe in their mouth, even women and children barely five years old being partial to the weed. The ornaments of the women consist of a profusion of beads worn as a necklace, mixed with colourless glass and oblong pieces of coarse cornelian; a thin plate of silver fixed on the head; and earrings as thick as or even thicker than those worn by the men, with a triangular plate of silver suspended from each, which remains in the direction of the shoulders.

The habitations of the Mishmees are hid in jungles, and are built apart from each other, as they do not congregate in villages. They are usually erected on slopes, resting on one side on the hill-face and on the other on poles driven into the ground. Those belonging to the chiefs are very long and about twelve feet in breadth. One side of each hut is partitioned off to exhibit the skulls of the animals on which the owner had in the course of his life feasted his friends, while the other is divided into smaller apartments, in all of which one or more hearths are always blazing. The house and its inmates are, for this reason, always black with dust and smoke, the more so as the latter are not over-fond of ablutions. At one time this people caused much trouble by their depredations, but they are now best known on the frontier as keen traders only, every man among them having converted himself into a petty merchant. Their country is, for the most part, very rugged and difficult to travel in; but they are never tired of moving about in their trading expeditions, and for many years no greater crime has been traced to them than kidnapping women and children, where they can get at them, to sell them into slavery. Some of them are clever manufacturers, and utilise the fibrous plants growing wild in their hills for the preparation of stiff cloths. One species of cloth made by them is so strong that it serves as a sort of armour in war; and every cloth they weave sells well, the Ábors being their principal customers. They are known as being sharp in their dealings generally, and most of them are deceitful also; and the practice of using poisoned arrows in fight has always been common with them. Exchange of dress, however, gives birth to, or is a sign of, amity; and by exchange of weapons the most deadly enemies become fast friends, and if one falls in fight it becomes the duty of the other to avenge his death and recover his skull. Polygamy prevails largely among all the tribes, the number of a man's wives being held to be the test of his wealth and consequence. The women are very comely, but mostly of indifferent character. Wives are, in fact, not expected to be chaste, and are not thought worse of when they are otherwise; and, as among the Meeris, the son of a Mishmee always succeeds to the use of his father's widows, his own mother only going over to the next of kin among the males. The religion of the race is confined to the propitiation of demons and sylvan deities, the most feared of all being the god of destruction; and pigs and fowls are sacrificed to them.

THE KHÁMPTIS.

Crossing the Brahmapootra we come to the Khámptis and the Singphos, both colonies of the Shán race of Burmáh, who came to Assam from the sources of the Irráwádi. They are found in and about Sudiyá, the extreme north-eastern corner of Assam, where the Khámptis are said to have settled in A.D. 1750. The Bor Khámptis of the Irráwádi, from whom they claim immediate descent, are a numerous and powerful people by whom the Burmese army is largely recruited, and the Assam branch of the tribe are also tall and well made. They were, however, not a very graceful race at the outset, and even now, though their intermarriage with the Assamese has somewhat softened and improved their features, their women are very plain-looking, if not ugly. They make themselves uglier by turning up their hair into a knot on the centre of the head, a fashion common to both sexes; but the natural profusion of their tresses necessarily makes the knots of the women bigger and therefore more hideous. The dress of both men and women is decent, the nether garments being a *dhoti* of chequered pattern, or silk, which the women wear as a petticoat. The upper clothing of the men is a tight-fitting jacket usually dyed blue, and a white turban; while the women wear a looser jacket and a coloured scarf over it. The ornaments in use are all made of metal and small glass beads. The arms of the men are the *dáo* for all offensive purposes, and a shield, some carrying China-made matchlocks also where they have got them. But they are not much given to martial pursuits at present. They are the most civilised of all the mountain tribes in Assam, and are everywhere very peacefully employed in field-work, house-building, working in metals, marketing, and the like; and are said to understand a little of reading and writing also. They rear pigs and fowls in abundance, and hold weekly markets to dispose of their surplus stocks, the articles usually consisting of pigs, fowls, eggs, dried fish, salt, ginger, onions, tobacco, and *dáos*. The currency of the country is the *dáo*, and also unwrought iron. The marketing is conducted in an orderly and business-like manner, without any of the haggling and driving a bargain so common in Hindu *bazárs*. The buyers and sellers are separated into groups for the sale of each article, so that the buyer has every variety of the article he requires exposed before him. In their field labours the men are much assisted by their wives, and the out-turn is ordinarily abundant. Their houses are always well and strongly built of sound timber, with raised floors and thatched roofs, and some of the buildings, especially their temples, are delicately carved. This finds work even for their chiefs, who also have apt hands for embroidery, and amuse themselves moreover by manufacturing silver pipes, brass bowls, and other nick-nacks of the same kind, which are said to be neatly made. The religion professed by the race is Buddhism, as it is understood in Burmáh; and their chief festivals have reference to the birth and death of Gautama. Polygamy is permitted, but seldom availed of; and the women have every liberty allowed to them, and are well-treated.

THE SINGPHOS.

The Singphos are a more powerful race than the Khámptis, nominally divided into twelve *gáums*, or clans, of whom three or four are considered to be the most influential, though they are all quite independent of each other, and never unite except in the prosecution of a common purpose. Each clan is, in fact, wholly governed by its chief, and acts separately for, with, or against the others as circumstances or inclination may direct. Much trouble was caused by all of them on the frontier at one time, and even now their life is not altogether peaceful, though they are catching civilisation quickly from the Khámptis. The men are somewhat better looking than the Khámptis, though having features of the same type, and are very athletic and capable of enduring great fatigue; but their women, who work with them, though actually of more pleasing features than the Khámpti women, very soon become coarse-looking from the hard labour devolving on them. The dress of both sexes is nearly the same with that of the Khámptis, and they wear their hair also after the same manner, in a knot on the crown of the head, except that the unmarried girls gather it in a roll resting on the back of the neck. Both men and women tattoo their limbs, the women more largely than the men, which disfigures them to a greater degree. The arms of the men, like those of the Khámptis, consist of the *dáo*, the shield, and the matchlock, and include in addition the crossbow and arrows; and their occupations, too, are very similar, the Singphos being only more partial to iron-smelting than to any other work. The *dáos* they make are very highly prized all over the frontier, and get rapid sale; and they also make their own apparel. The country they occupy is low and extremely fertile, and rice, sugar-cane, and corn thrive well upon it; but, cultivation having long been neglected in it, owing to the original predatory habits of the people, it is at present largely overgrown with jungle. The religion of the people is Buddhism, of the same shape as of the Khámptis; and they believe also in malignant spirits, who are propitiated with sacrifices. Polygamy is extensively practised, and, besides the wives married, slaves are retained, the offspring of both having equal rights. The law of succession is peculiar, too, in another way—it gives to the eldest son all the landed property of the father, to the youngest all his personal property, while the rest inherit nothing; and this division is made without reference to the mother's status or nationality. The dead are buried, and the bodies of the chiefs are kept in state often for two or more years, in a coffin which is surrounded with the insignia of the rank held by them in life; and the process of decomposition leaves nothing beyond the bones to inter.

THE NÁGÁS.

The Nágás lie to the south-west of the Khámptis and the Singphos, being scattered all over the mountain ridge that divides Assam from Munipore.

The word "Nágá" means a serpent, but it is not pretended that the Nágás are of serpent or Scythic descent. The name was more probably given to them originally as being best expressive of their character, for of all wild tribes they are held to be the most subtle and treacherous. There are about a dozen septs of them, who differ considerably from each other in several respects, each having some distinct peculiarity of its own and often a distinct language. Those of the upper ranges are generally light-coloured and handsome, and their women pretty, though beauty of form is not the rule of the hills; but those of the lower ranges, such as the Lotáh Nágás and others, are dark, dirty, and squat. The differences in character also are equally prominent, for, while the Rengmá Nágás are spoken of as being good-natured, peaceful, and honest, the Lotáhs are known as unsocial and sulky, and the Ángámis as contentious, vindictive, and perfidious. The Nágás *par excellence* are the last, whose name *Ángámi*, or the "unconquered," is their boast. They live high up the mountains, and have always distinguished themselves as caterans and murderers, and also for being perpetually at feud with each other, their feuds going down from generation to generation. Their villages are accordingly planned for everyday defence and stockaded as hill-forts, from which barbarous onslaughts are made, in which neither age nor sex is spared. They gave a world of trouble to the

Government by the many plundering inroads they made on the peaceful tribes occupying the foot of their hills; and several expeditions had to be sent against them, commencing from 1835. In 1865, the location of a special officer in their hills was determined upon, and the country taken under direct management, after which its history was rather uneventful for a long time, though never altogether peaceful. Subsequently some outrages were perpetrated in 1879, in connexion with an attempt to dislodge the British authority from the hills, and culminated in the murder of the special officer, Mr. Damant, and his escort, which led to an expedition being undertaken against the savages by General Nation, and to their punishment. Peace has since been ostensibly restored; but it is hardly to be supposed that it will be long preserved. The bellicose disposition of the race has not yet been mastered, and what seems calculated to master it in the future even more than Government interference is tea-planting, the operations connected with which are gradually spreading British rule over the immense wastes now held by these people, the limits of which are likely to be extended in the end to Munipore on the south, and on the east to the Pátkoi range and the borders of Burmáh and China. The Nágás are carrying on a most profitable business with the tea gardens, and those so engaged have already been partially humanised, at the same time that their occupation has forced them to neglect their internal bickerings.

The Nágás are a fine, stalwart race, though inferior in *physique* as compared with the tribes inhabiting the north of the Brahmapootra, having smaller bones and much less of muscular development. Their faces are lozenge-shaped, features flat, eyes small, complexion dark; and of hair they have none in the shape of beard, whisker, or moustache, while that on the head is cut short and trained to stand erect. But, despite these drawbacks, their carriage is dignified, and they have over all a wild expression peculiar to them, which distinguishes them from all other tribes in their vicinity. The females are short and waistless, but not necessarily ungainly, though they are too hard-worked to retain any shade of comeliness long, having every employment, apart from fighting, hunting, and traffic, saddled on them. There is no clothing for either sex in the higher elevations, and hence some imagine that the name Nágá may, perhaps, have been derived from the word "Lungá," or naked. At the foot of the hills the limbs are usually covered with a small piece of cloth dyed with indigo, a larger piece of coarse cloth being also used for covering the body when needed; while nearer the tea gardens the men wear kilts of different patterns and colours, and the women picturesque petticoats, and a cotton *chádur* thrown across the back and chest. They are very fond of ornaments at all places, and both males and females go loaded with them, the trinkets consisting of necklaces, bracelets, and armlets, made mainly of cowries, and more rarely of greenish beads which are particularly prized. What the Nágá most of all delights in, however, are his weapons, which are his constant companions, awake and sleeping. These are: the *dáo*, or battle-axe, the spear or javelin, and the shield —for he never uses the bow and arrows. The Ángámis have also long known the use of firearms, of which they have got a considerable supply. Fighting and hunting, however, are not their sole occupations at the present day. They understand the advantages of trading, and frequently come down to the markets of Assam and Cáchár heavily laden with ivory, wax, and cloths manufactured from the nettle-fibre, in exchange for which they receive salt, brassware, and shells, and, by preference, matchlocks and gunpowder if they can get them. Their only other occupations are dancing and debauch, both of which are sometimes, not always, shared in by their women. The war-dance in particular is performed by the men alone, with spear and hatchet in hand, while all the circumstances of battle are acted, namely, the advance, retreat, wielding of weapons, and defence with the shield, accompanied by terrific howls and war-whoops.

As the Nágás are not a migratory people, like the other hillmen around them, their villages are stationary and unchanging, and those marked in Rennel's Maps of 1764 are still to be found. Some of them are very large, containing so many as five hundred houses, and there are none which have less than fifty. The houses are built after a peculiar fashion, having the eaves down to the ground, while one gable-end forms the door to enter by. Every family has a separate house, and each house generally contains two rooms, one for sleeping in, and the other for all other purposes, including the custody of pigs and fowls. The accommodation is necessarily straitened, and the unmarried young men of the family have to sleep out of it, all the bachelors of a village being accommodated in one common building, furnished with a series of bamboo beds covered with mats. In this house are also exhibited the spoils of the chase and the implements of war belonging to the community; and it is further used as the village inn, in which travellers from other villages are allowed to put up. The separation of the sexes in youth, if intended, is not, however, actually very rigidly enforced, young men and women having every facility given to them to become well acquainted with each other; and when they have made up their minds to marry they are at once united, the only form gone through being the execution of a contract of union by both parties, unattended by any religious ceremony whatever. Presents are then made by the bridegroom to the family of the bride, and there is a grand feast given to the whole village, in return for which the villagers have to build a house for the accommodation of the youthful pair. Divorces and remarriages are both allowed and freely availed of, and open infidelity is necessarily not of frequent occurrence.

As a rule the Nágá woman is a model of labour and industry, and is mainly valued on that account. She does everything the husband will not, and he considers it effeminate to do anything but fight, hunt, and cheat. The cultivation labours are all performed by the wife, the crops raised consisting of rice, cotton, and tobacco, as well as several kinds of vegetables. She also weaves, both with cotton and with nettle-fibres, and manufactures salt from the many salt-springs in the country, though she is not able to make it at less cost than is charged for the salt sent up from Bengal. The tending of cows, goats, pigs, and fowl likewise devolves on her in most places, and she of course cooks and performs every other household work besides. One curious way of cooking with some clans is thus described in Owen's *Nágá Tribes*:—"Their manner of cooking is performed in joints of bamboos, introduced into which are as much rice, chillies, and meat, with water, as each will hold and can be thrust tightly in by the aid of a stick. A couple of bamboos placed on the ground, with a third connecting them at the top horizontally, constitutes a fire-place, against which those holding the food rest.

By continually turning the bamboos the food becomes well roasted, and is then served out on leaves from a neighbouring tree." Neither milk nor any preparation thereof is appreciated by the Nágás generally, but they eat animals of all kinds, including rats, snakes, monkeys, tigers, and elephants; and the roast dog in particular is regarded as a great delicacy. Another article equally prized is a liquor manufactured from fermented rice, which is drunk by both sexes in great quantities; they are inveterate smokers also, and are especially fond of the oil of tobacco, which they mix with water and drink.

The Nágás have no kind of internal government, and acknowledge no supreme authority. If spoken to on the subject they plant their javelin on the ground and declare that to be their Rájáh, and that they will have none other. The *Gáon Boorá*, or elder of the village, has some authority conceded to him; but it is very moderate, and is often resisted and defied. A council of elders is suffered to adjust petty disputes and disagreements, but only in the way of arbitration. There is no constituted authority lodged anywhere in the community; every man doing what he likes and is able to perform. The Nágá is by nature fierce as the tiger, and matters are necessarily made worse from the total want of control over his passions. His other vices are drunkenness and thieving, in the latter of which he glories, though it is held very dishonourable to be discovered in the act. His religion consists in the worship of a plurality of deities, or good and evil spirits, to whom sacrifices are made, and in the belief in omens, by which his conduct is mainly guided. The chief religious festival is called the Genná, a Sabbath extended generally over two or three days and nights, when all the inhabitants of the village celebrating it live in complete isolation from others, sacrificing and drinking, but not permitting any one to witness their debaucheries. There is no fixed time for this ceremony, which is frequently repeated in the course of the year—that is, whenever it is considered necessary to make propitiatory offerings to their gods. The dead among them are buried at the doors of their own houses, and the spear and *dáo* of the warrior are always buried with him.

THE CÁCHÁRESE.

The district which has suffered most from the Nágá raids is Cáchár, which, within a small confined area, holds several tribes pushed into it from different directions. Of these the most important are: the Cáchárese, the minor Nágá tribes, the Meckirs, and the Kookies.

The Cáchárese are a large race whose proper name is Rangtsá, and their original country that situated to the north-east of Assam. They were at one time limited to Cáchár, and still form the dominant class of the district, but are now also scattered all over Assam; and even the Hájongs of Mymensing are held to be a branch of the same family. They are a fine hardy race, quiet, industrious, and thriving, and have strongly marked Mongolian features. Both men and women wear the hair long, but even full-grown men have no beard or whiskers. The primary divisions of the race are two—namely, the Hazái, or people of the plains, and the Purbutteáhs, or people of the hills. The former profess to be Hindus, but eat pigs and fowls, and even sacrifice them to their gods, with the exception of the Seroniáh, or "the purified," who have adopted Hindu prejudices in regard to food in their integrity, and the Shargiah, or "the heavenly," who border on Thibet and Bootán, and have accepted Llámáism with all its conventionalities. The chief occupation of the race is cultivation; but, while the dwellers of the plains cultivate with the plough, those of the hills do so with the hoe only. The jungles among which the Purbutteáhs live are mainly of bamboos, and these, being cut down and set on fire, leave a coating of ashes on the ground, which is the only manure used to fertilise it. The soil below the ashes is then turned up with the hoe, and the seeds to be sown are dropped in—paddy, sugar-cane, cotton, and tobacco being all sown together in the same ground. Each plot of ground is cultivated only for two years, after which it is left untouched for from seven to ten years, on the expiration of which it is considered to be once more fit for cultivation.

The villages of the Cáchárese comprise from twenty to a hundred houses, each family having a separate dwelling for itself. The bachelors live apart from their families, in a large house in the centre of every village, which is called the *Dekhá chang*, or the warriors' house; but opportunities are given to them to consort with the maidens, and marriage still preserves the primitive form of abduction. When the lovers have agreed to unite their fortunes together, the bridegroom proceeds with his friends to the house of the bride to get forcible possession of her person. Her friends, affecting surprise, run out to the rescue in haste, and there is a stubborn mock-fight between the parties with no violence committed on either side. Eventually the bridegroom's party proves successful, upon which he gives a feast to the discomfited friends of the bride, and conciliates her father, who is supposed to be mightily incensed, by a money present, which completes the ceremony. The religion of the race, we have already said, is an affectation of Hinduism *minus* its food restrictions. Except the very orthodox, all classes eat meat of all kinds, beef only excepted; they also drink spirits, though in no immoderate degree, and are not unacquainted with the use of opium. The general intelligence of the race is not much to speak of, though the Hazáis affect to have got educated by their connexion with the Assamese. Diseases are believed to arise from preternatural agency, and in place of doctors they have *rojáhs*, or exorcists, to cure them. Witchcraft is also believed in, and the *rojáh* assists here too in removing the spell.

THE MEEKIRS.

The Meekirs came originally from the jungles marked in the maps as Toolarám Senáputty's country, and, like the Cácharese, are divided into classes, namely, the hill and plain Meekirs respectively. They are physically much inferior to the Cácharese, and even the hill Meekirs are not warriors. But, if cowardly, they have the credit of being very laborious, and raise rice and cotton in abundance, the latter of which they sell to advantage. The only weapon they carry is the *dáo*, of which no use is made except for cultivation and wood cutting. Their dress consists of two pieces of cotton cloth dyed with red stripes and sewn together like a bag, with apertures left for the head and arms; and this is put on in the manner of a shirt. They build their houses on high *máchâns*, or platforms, and the buildings are always large, being made to hold some thirty or forty persons, often of different families, who sleep together almost in a state of nudity. The chief food of the tribe consists of rice, pigs, and goats; but they refrain from eating cows, more from prudential than religious motives. They also delight in spirituous liquors, which are often drunk to excess; but they are peaceful in their cups, and disturbances seldom occur. Of religion their idea is indefinite, though they affect to have become converted to Hinduism. The objects worshipped are the Sun and Moon, and large rocks and forest trees, which are considered to be the abodes of invisible deities. Animal sacrifices are made at these places and offered up along with boiled rice. For marriage they have no religious ceremony. A bargain is made between the parties proposing to be united, and a contract entered into which makes them man and wife, a feast being given in commemoration of the event. Polygamy is discountenanced, but not expressly forbidden; and widows are allowed to remarry.

THE KOOKIES.

The Kookies are a numerous race whose proper limits have not been defined even to this day. Their original settlements seem to have been in the hill recesses to the south of the Hylákandy valley, a wild and difficult country of large extent, whence they have branched out northwards into Hill Tipperáh, and southwards into Chittagong. The tribes occupying such a large territory are of course various, and are known under different names in different places, such as Lunctás, Chuckmás, Tipperáhs, Reángs, Lusháis, etc, all living independent of each other, and each ruled over by its own separate chief. The appellation "Kookie" is equally unknown to all of them, having been given to them by the inhabitants of Eastern Bengal: for their whole race they have no common name, and are content to call one another by the names of their different clans. But their general characteristics are very similar in all places, and they are easily distinguishable by them from other tribes. They are all of stout and muscular make, though of a short size, and have a dark complexion, flat nose, and small eyes. Of some the legs are disproportionately short and the arms disproportionately long; and the face, which in every case is as broad as it is long, is among some tribes round, but among others nearly square. The women of all tribes are equally ungainly and filthy, and more squat even than the men; but they are at the same time very strong and lusty. The dress of the different tribes varies to some extent according to taste and locality; but there is not much room for variation where the general fashon is to go naked. According to their own traditions the Kookies and the Mughs, or Joomeáhs, are of the same parentage, born of the same father by different mothers. The mother of the Kookies dying first, during the infancy of her son, the child was brought up by his stepmother, who gave him no clothing, and so he came to be called *Lunctá*, or "the naked." Where any dress is worn, the women have a small blue cloth round the loins, reaching from below the navel to the knee, and another cloth thrown over the shoulders, while the men have their *dhotis* and *merzáis*, and a cloth tied round the head which stands for a turban. The women wear no head-dress at any place, but cultivate a luxuriant crop of hair instead of it. The ornaments worn are necklaces, armlets and bracelets made of brass which are very massy, and earrings. The arms of the warriors are the *dáo*, the bow and arrows, and the spear, a shield being occasionally used in addition for defence. Strings are also worn by them around the neck, both as ornament and armour; and tufts of goat-hair dyed red are worn on the thighs. The distinctive mark of the Tipperáhs is a large quill stuck on the back of the head, from which red-coloured goat-hair is hung out in streamers.

The Kookies in Cáchár are divided into two primary septs called the "old" and the "new." The "old" are subdivided into three clans, of whom the most considerable in numbers are the Rhangkol, who are very powerful men physically, and very steady labourers, both for working and carrying. They dress decently, and are fond of ornaments; but, like the rest of their race, neither wash their bodies nor their clothes, and are eaten up with skin diseases. They have no chiefs, but every village has a headman with limited powers. Their notions of religion are mainly borrowed from the Assamese, and are vague;

but marriage is a religious ceremony with them, and always requires the presence of the *Ghálim*, or priest. There is no polygamy among them, and widows have the same liberty as widowers to remarry.

The "new" Kookies were driven into Cáchár by the Lunctás within the recollection of the present generation, some thirty years ago. They are divided into four clans, each having a rájáh, or chief, of its own, who is entitled to receive one out of each brood of pigs or fowls, one quarter of every animal killed in the chase, one tusk of every elephant slain, and one basket of rice from each of his subjects. He is also entitled to receive free labour from each man for four days in the year, and has the privilege of adjusting their quarrels and differences with the assistance of a council of elders and of laws peculiar to the tribe, his decision being final in every case. The religion of the tribe recognises an all-powerful deity named Puthen, who has a wife, a son, and a daughter-in-law; and, in addition to them, there are household gods, to whom sacrifices are made.

The Tipperáhs are Kookies who own allegiance to the Rájáh of Tipperáh, paying him an annual *nuzzur*, and *abwábs* on marriage and other occasions. They are fairer than the other tribes, some of them being hardly darker than a swarthy European, but are not distinguishable from the rest in any other respect. They pretend to be Hindus, but have no restrictions of caste, and eat almost any kind of food, and from the hands of any person. Pigs, fowls, and pigeons are reared by them; but they keep no oxen, which they do not eat nor know any other use of.

The most powerful of the Kookie tribes are the Lusháis, who are also the most easterly; and it is on account of their wars and raids mainly that the other septs have been forced forward into British territory in the directions indicated. The quarrels of the Lusháis, like those of the Nágás, are incessant, and, as they always prefer to surprise their enemies instead of attacking them openly, however strong their own party might be, there is no option left to those who are attacked but to fly before them, since their main object is not so much to plunder as to kill or take slaves. Proceeding on a foray, they will march in the night with the stealthy pace of the jackal, in the most profound silence, and on being overtaken by day will so conceal themselves among trees as to remain unperceived by persons passing under them, waiting in ambush till the time for surprise arrives. The only notice given of an attack is the shout by which it is commenced, and those who cannot fly are either killed or carried off. After victory the assailants retire, taking away the heads of the slain and their slaves, the former to be used in certain ceremonies performed at the funerals of their chiefs, and for being exhibited as trophies. But, if they are defeated, they go back to their homes as silently as they came, and live in disgrace till their failure is retrieved. The one well understood law with all of them is that blood can only be wiped out with blood; and, if the murderer be a tiger, the Lushái will rush after him to kill him, and will never be satisfied till he has been killed, cooked, and eaten. Nay, if a man is killed by the fall of a tree, his friends will cut up the tree into chips, or burn it till it is reduced to ashes. The trouble caused on the frontier by a race so vindictive was necessarily great, and, in 1871-72, the Government had to send a rather strong party against them to repress their inroads, which was successful to this extent, that some of the raiding chiefs were punished and accepted the terms that were dictated to them.

The general character of the race is that they are nomadic but gregarious; frequently shifting their grounds, but not so migratory as the Mughs. The latter never remain on the same spot for more than two years; but the Kookie settlements are seldom changed before the expiration of four or five years. Their villages, called *khoodáhs*, are therefore always better formed and finished than those of their neighbours. They are usually posted on the steepest and most inaccessible hills, and are fortified with bamboo palisades, while the passages to them are guarded day and night, in peace and war. Precautions of this sort are necessary on account of the aggressive character of the race and the outrages they perpetrate, which invite reprisals. The houses in the villages are usually well made, and are raised on platforms of bamboos some six feet from the ground, and ranged in rows on each side of a street. Their cultivation patches also are very carefully arranged, but the work on these devolves mostly on their women. The men are all hunters and warriors, while the women work on the fields, an occupation from which no rank exempts them, the wife of a chief working alongside of the wife of his vassal. The process of cultivation is *jooming*, and the crops raised are rice and other grains of various sorts, roots, vegetables, tobacco, and cotton. The grains and vegetables form the chief food of the people, besides which they are fond of eating flesh of all kinds, and rear pigs and poultry. They also make their own fermented liquors and spirits, but do not drink intemperately, and are seldom seen intoxicated. They are more fond of tobacco, which is smoked not only by men and women, but also by children; and, in common with the Nágás, they drink the oil of tobacco mixed with water. Of the cotton raised by them the best portion is sold to the Bengali *bepáris* by barter for fowls, each fowl being considered equivalent to its weight of cotton. A prodigious quantity of honey is also found in their forests, but they do not know how to separate it from the wax of the comb. In some places they are so rude that they still kindle fire by rubbing two pieces of wood together, and use the ashes of the bamboo as a substitute for salt. Their greatest of all virtues is valour, and the only accomplishments worth acquiring are: first, a knowledge of the military tactics practised by themselves, and, after it, thieving—the most contemptible of men, however, being, as with the Nágás, a detected thief. An oath taken by a Kookie is always held sacred; but it is very seldom that he will take any, and never except on very serious occasions.

The women of the Kookies, as among the Nágás, are only valued for the amount of labour they perform. The manner of obtaining a wife is either by paying a price for her, or, in the old Jewish fashion, by serving for her in bondage for a term of years; but no great value is placed on her rectitude. Cases of adultery and seduction are inquired into and punished, the punishment resting with the husband or father from whose charge the girl may have been seduced; but, on the other hand, all the women of a village, married or unmarried, are available to the chief at his will, and no stigma attaches to those who are favoured by him. Polygamy is not permitted; but there is no objection to retaining concubines in addition to a wife. The marriage arrangements on behalf of the female are usually made by her father, and his inquiries in regard to her lover are best answered when the answer is that he is a great warrior, a good hunter, and an expert thief. The proofs demanded, and which have to be shown, are the heads of the enemies slain by him, the heads of the game he may have killed, and the goods in his house that were stolen. If these are forthcoming, the arrangements are at once concluded. The idea of religion among all tribes is very similar to that entertained by the "new" Kookies of Cáchár, except that the wilder Kookies believe more largely in spirits having charge of their forests, hills, and rivers, than in household deities, and that the best sacrifice a man can make to them is the heads of his enemies. Their idea of Paradise represents a happy hunting-ground, where rice grows spontaneously, and game abounds as the heritage of the man who has killed the largest number of his enemies in life, the people killed by him attending on him as his slaves. The chief end and object of life with the Kookie is, in fact, to kill his enemies, and there can be no greater virtue or glory than to do so. Diseases are believed to be inflicted by malevolent spirits who have to be pacified; and there is no other treatment for them. Some tribes burn their dead, along with different kinds of eatables given to the corpse; others bury them; but the burial day comes round once only in the year, and till its return each body is kept by in a shed, all the bodies being buried together when the day returns.

The Cossyáhs.

Adjoining the Kookies and the Meekirs are the Cossyáhs, usually called Khásiáhs in all the later official reports and other documents relating to them, but whom we prefer to call by their old name, if only to distinguish them from the Khásiáhs of Kumáon and Gurhwál. They are an athletic race of mountaineers, who are reputed to have frequently laid the plains of Assam under contribution in former times; but they are very well behaved at present, though still fond of martial exercises, and may be said to have become partially civilised as compared with the races by whom they are surrounded. The men have no hair on their face beyond a miserable wiry moustache, but make a good appearance notwithstanding; and the women are decidedly handsome, though not very cleanly. What is yet more remarkable of the race is that they are full of life and spirits, and are always singing, screaming, whistling, and running about, having great powers of industry though they are capricious in exerting them. The dress of the men consists of a *dhoti* and a long shirt without sleeves, over which a *chádur* is also occasionally worn; while the women wear a shapeless mantle of striped cotton cloth tied into a knot across the breast. The martial dress of the men substitutes a sleeveless tunic of lòng cloth for the shirt, the arms carried being a shield of buffalo hide or brass, a powerful two-handed sword, the bow and arrows, and a javelin. The use of poisoned arrows against wild beasts is common; but it speaks much for the manhood of the race that they have never been known to use them against their fellow creatures. Their common food comprises rice, millet, maize, *kochu*, and arrowroot, all of which are raised by themselves; besides which they also eat flesh of all kinds, including that of the leopard, and are especially fond of pork and dried fish. They do not drink milk, nor make any use of *ghee*, and are not partial to intoxicating liquors; but they are excessively fond of *pán*, a large supply of which they carry about with them and chew incessantly. This dyes their teeth and lips red, and they pride themselves on the dirty habit by saying that "dogs and Bengalis only have white teeth." Their progress in the industrial arts has not been very great, and being unacquainted with weaving they are obliged to get their clothes from other tribes.

The tribal divisions of the race are many, but they all combine to form a confederacy which, though not subject to a common superior, is yet amenable in some degree to the control of each clan. Their domestic relations are in several respects very peculiar. The husband does not take his wife home, but goes over to live with her at her father's house, almost like a retainer in her service. At one time polyandry was very prevalent among them, but that has now been supplanted by a great facility of divorce. The marriage tie is so loose that separation is signified simply by the exchange of five cowries, and is constant, the children in every case abiding with the mother. The law of inheritance is equally curious, sister's children being recognised by it as heirs in preference to one's own sons. The religion of the race acknowledges the existence of a Supreme Being, but more reverence is paid by them to the inferior spirits believed to reside in their hills and groves. They have great faith also in omens, their divination being drawn principally from the breaking of eggs. Over the dead there is a carousal continued for several days, in which feasts, dances, mock fights, and fairs figure prominently, a furious howling being also kept on. The dead are burnt, but not necessarily at the time of death, being often preserved a long time for a more convenient season for disposing of them. There are some monolithic monuments in their hills, such as are also found in various parts of Europe and Western Asia, consisting of large flat circular slabs to sit upon, and also of long upright pillars of irregular shape. These are believed to be monuments raised over the dead; but it has not been ascertained by whom and under what circumstances they were raised.

THE GÁROS.

To the west of the Cossyáhs are the Gáros, who inhabit the range of hills which divide Assam from Bengal Proper. This tract has been under British domination from 1822, but till recently the control of the Government extended only over the zemindáry and tributary Gáros, not over the independent clans who occupy the summits of the hills. The raids committed by these on their lowland neighbours were frequent, and this forced an expedition being undertaken against them in 1866, which finally resulted in the formation of the Gáro Hill district, which has been as successful as the similar arrangements in other places.

The older writers speak of the Gáros and Cossyáhs as one people; but this they are not, though there is certainly much similarity between them. The Gáros are of shorter make and harsher features than the Cossyáhs; but they are stout limbed and of great bodily strength like them, and a Gáro woman will carry over the hills a load which a Bengal cooly will with difficulty carry across the plains. The southern Gáros have the advantage of being stouter and better formed than their northern neighbours; but they are all equally ugly, and even their women are unlovely, though the girls are good humoured and have very musical voices. The temperament of the race is well spoken of. They are lively, goodnatured, hospitable, frank and honest, and very truthful. They are also affectionate fathers and kind husbands, and their respect for their women is evinced by all property-right being conceded to them. Among the evil customs prevalent amidst them, the immolation of human victims (who were always Bengalis) in honour of the dead was at one time very common; and they are still stanch slaveholders on a large scale, about two-fifths of the entire population of the country being dependent on the remaining three-fifths. The slaves are called *Nakal*, and the free men *Nákobá;* and the distinction between them is jealously preserved, though otherwise the slaves are not ill-treated, being well fed and well cared for, while they in return are devoted to their masters. The dress of the Gáros is very scanty. The males live almost wholly nude, their sole garment being a narrow strip of cloth worn as a girdle round the waist, which is passed from behind through the legs and brought up in the front. The female dress is nearly the same, consisting of a piece of cloth less than a foot in breadth wound round the loins, while all the other parts of the body are left bare. The ornaments worn by the women are earrings and bead necklaces; while many go altogether unadorned, accepting the verdict of the poet that beauty when unadorned is adorned the most. They eat all kinds of food, including cats, dogs, frogs, and snakes; and rear kine, goats, swine, fowls, and ducks. Like the

Nágás, Cossyáhs, and others, they abhor milk, and call it diseased matter. It is said that they are particularly fond of eating puppies, which they dress in a manner peculiar to themselves. The animal is fed with as large a quantity of rice as it will take, and is then roasted alive. When the roast is done, the puppy is cut up and eaten, the rice in its stomach being regarded as a delicacy. Their passion for drink is so great that liquor is given even to infants to swallow; and their excess in the indulgence is often productive of bloody brawls, which are more frequent, however, among the southern than among the northern Gáros, the latter being provoked by drink only to more dancing and music.

The houses of the Gáros are called *changs*, and are from thirty to one-hundred-and-fifty feet in length, and from ten to forty in breadth. They are roofed with thatch, or with mats of long grass, and propped up with *sál* timbers, of which the beams also are made. The sides are constructed of hollow bamboos cut open and woven like a mat. Every house is divided into two parts, the upper and the lower, the latter being allotted to cattle and poultry. The upper story is subdivided into distinct enclosures for the owner and his wife and their unmarried daughters and other children generally, while the unmarried sons are housed separately in a bachelors' hall, with which every village is provided. The total number of houses in a village is about twenty, and they are almost all of them substantially built. One peculiarity to be noted is that the villages or clans are divided into *Máháris*, or motherhoods, particular Máháris being especially connected with and intermarrying into each other. A man's sister marries in the family from which he derives his wife; his son may marry a daughter of that sister, and, as male heirs do not inherit, the son-in-law, succeeding his father-in-law in right of his wife, gets his father's sister, who is his wife's mother, as an additional wife to live with. The marriage process is also peculiar. The selection is made by the girl, and the male can make no advances till the female's wishes are known. The consent of the parents of the parties is implied, with this proviso—that, if the old people refuse, they can be beaten into compliance. After these preliminaries have been settled, the female and her party again take the initiative and proceed to the house of the bridegroom to secure him, while he pretends to run away from them. He is quickly caught, and, in spite of resistance offered, is married, amidst lamentations and counterfeit grief both on his part and on the part of his parents. The ceremony is completed by the sacrifice of a cock and a hen, when the piteous howls of the bridegroom and his party subside under the usual debaucheries of a feast. Her husband thus secured, the wife usually becomes a good helpmate to him, sharing in all the labours of husbandry, besides being his guardian angel at home. One couple usually cultivates from three to four *beegáhs* of land a year, and three crops are raised on it in rotation, namely, the *áousdhán*, cotton, and millet. The chief productions of the Gáro hills are: cotton, *áousdhán*, maize, millet, chillies, and yams. It is on cotton chiefly that the people depend for those necessaries of life which their hills will not yield. They are, besides, good workers in iron and bell-metal, and make *koráhs* or *thállees* of the latter which are much prized in Bengal. Their implements of husbandry are: a hoe, a *dáo*, and a battle-axe, which is used for all purposes. No Gáro is ever seen without the axe, except when a spear is substituted for it to answer any especial purpose. The wilder Gáros protect their villages in war time by stockading them, and by blocking up all approaches to them with felled trees, besides which *pánjees*, or sharp bamboo spikes, are thickly planted, and so deep that they cannot be extracted, the only way to remove them being to shave them even with the ground. The religion of the people recognises a great god named Kishijee, the character given to whom is very like that of the Hindu god Siva; but they make no images of him, and have no temples to worship him in. What they are commonly seen to adore is the bamboo adorned with flowers and tufts of cotton thread. They burn their dead, and bury the ashes exactly where the pile was kindled, over which a hut is often erected in which the wearing apparel of the deceased is deposited.

CHAPTER IV.

TRIBES ON THE EASTERN FRONTIER.

THE chief tribes on the eastern frontier are the Kookies, to whom we have already referred, the Joomeáhs or Mughs, the Kheongthás, who are so like the Joomeáhs in all respects as to require no separate notice, and the Shindoos; and, lower down, the Khoomeás, the Koos, the Mroos or Mroo Khyens, and the Khyens. All the races are extremely migratory. They occupy small hamlets surrounded by bamboo stockades perched on the top of almost inaccessible hills; but where one sees a village at one time he finds nothing but a jungle six months after, the people inhabiting the village having moved off perhaps to half a day's, or a whole day's journey thence, transporting the very name of the village with their huts. In character some of the tribes are exceedingly inoffensive, while others are the very reverse of it, of which latter description are the Lusháis, Shindoos, and Koos, who are only known for their plundering expeditions and the outrages they perpetrate.

THE JOOMEÁHS.

The Joomeáhs, or Mughs, are understood to be the aboriginal inhabitants of Arracan, but now occupy in great numbers the hill-tracts of Chittagong, or rather that portion of them which is known by the name of the *Kápás Mahal*, or the cotton districts. They are called *Joomeáhs* because they cultivate by burning, the word *joom* in their language meaning "to burn." The plough is never used by them, and, in fact, they never cultivate land even enough for a plough to operate upon. They cut the jungle on their hill-sides and then set fire to it, the ashes being spread over and dug into the ground to manure it, after which the seeds are sown in the same manner as by other wild tribes generally. The personal appearance of the race is very like that of the Chinese, and especially distinguished by high and broad cheek bones, flat noses, and oblique eyes. Their forms are short, but well made and athletic, and their colour is of the mulatto kind. The hair of both sexes is glossy and black, and they are equally proud of its quality. The women wear it parted in the middle and tied in a knot at the back of the head; while the men put on a kind of turban of white cloth, which is entwined with their hair. The dress of the women consists of a cloth tightly bound round the bosom and flowing to the feet, with a large outer covering thrown over the whole person reaching to the knees; while that of the men is composed of one cloth wound round the middle and another thrown over the shoulders. The only ornaments worn by the women are thick earrings of various designs, to make room for which the lobes of their ears are widely perforated, those of the men being similarly bored to put in their cigars. The huts of the race are made of bamboos raised on piles several feet above the ground; each house being occupied by one family only, excluding the bachelors, who have a common dwelling allowed to them in every village. Their ordinary food is boiled rice and fish; but animals are also eaten, and nothing from the smallest to the biggest is indifferent to them. Both sexes smoke and chew tobacco; and they are also fond of *pán*, but do not drink much habitually. They are reputed to be very long-lived, and retain their strength and faculties to a great age; and altogether they are much less wild than the races by whom they are surrounded. The rich among them burn, while the poor bury, their dead, and with both a funeral is the occasion of mirth and rejoicing, which frequently end in dissipation and excess.

THE SHINDOOS.

The Shindoos occupy the forest tract between the valley of the Irráwádi and Arracan, to the east of the boundary range, the Lushái Kookies residing on its west. Numerically they are less strong than several races living near them, notably than the Khoomeás; but they are held in greater dread all over the frontier, even the Khoomeás being afraid of them. Their raids into Chittagong were at one time very frequent, the chief object always held in view by them being the capture of slaves. The villages proceeded against were invariably attacked at night and set on fire, and of those of the inhabitants who could not escape the males were killed and the females and children were carried off. These outrages have now been greatly checked; but the character of the race has not yet very materially improved. Their houses are built on raised platforms and are generally well made, bamboos or timber being used in their construction according to the wealth of the owners, and the thatching being of grass. They cultivate also with industry, and raise all the grains usually grown in jungly hills, such as maize, *bazrá*, hill-rice, yams, *kudoos*, ginger, *til*, linseed, cotton, and sugar-cane. They are rich too in pigs and poultry, but are more fond of dogs as food, and eat all sorts of game, including elephants. The arms used by the warriors are bows and arrows, short spears, and shields made of buffalo-hide. Muskets are also prized, and many have been secured and are often very mischievously used, the position occupied by them being too remote for any very effective control being exercised over them. Wives amongst them are always purchased, and polygamy is widely prevalent, almost every man having from two to four wives. Their religion is Buddhism, but so corrupted as to be hardly recognisable. The dead are buried by them in a supine posture, with the head to the east; and with the warrior are buried his weapons and his gongs.

THE KHOOMEÁS.

The Khoomeás occupy the country on both banks of the Koladyne river, from Thánnáh Koladyne to the mouth of the Sullá Kheong, and form the largest and most important of all the wild tribes in that direction. They are divided into many classes, of whom the most powerful are the Khoongchoo, Khoong, Ánoo, and Yeasing. The primary occupation of all of them is agriculture; besides which they also manufacture cloths, spears, and gunpowder; and all, or nearly all of them, practise dacoity. Their principal arm is the musket; but spears and shields are also used. Each tribe has its own chief, the confederate chiefs together representing the sovereign power.

THE KOOS.

The Koos inhabit the mountainous regions near the sources of the Lemroo and its principal feeder the Peng Kheong. They are near neighbours to the Khoomeás, and differ little from them in habits, but exceed them in barbarity. They are extremely wild, and are always at feud, either among themselves or with the other tribes about them. They have little or no clothing, but canes slit up in two and painted red are wrapped round the stomach as a protection in war. Their arms are the musket, the spear, and the bow and arrows. One striking peculiarity to be noted of them is that they drink the blood of animals ; and a well approved custom with them on festive occasions is to tie a bull or *gyál* (wild ox) to a stake, and to pierce him with spears, after which bamboo cups are applied to the wounds, from which men, women, and children drink the warm blood with great gusto.

THE MROOS.

The Mroos occupy the country north of the junction of the Saeng Kheong with the Lemroo. They are a quiet and inoffensive race, largely given to cultivation. The males frequently go naked, or have only a rag fastened in front below the loins, except in the cold weather when a cloak also is occasionally thrown over the body. The dress of the females is a dark blue cotton gown fastened at the neck and descending to the knees. Persons labouring under palsy, ulcers, leprosy, and other incurable diseases, are viewed by them as outcasts, and are not permitted to reside in the same place with the rest, a separate village being assigned to them, in which, however, they are well cared for and supported.

THE KHYENS.

The last tribe we shall notice are the Khyens, who inhabit the mountains between Arracan and Ává. They are very dissimilar to the Mughs, but resemble the Mroos so much that the two have been held by several writers to be only different tribes of the same race, which is highly probable. The Khyens live for the most part in the thickest retreats of their forests, and, being erratic in their habits, are constantly going about in parties, and pitch their tents wherever they can find fertile spots to cultivate. Their devotion to cultivation is greater even than that of the Mroos, and they raise large supplies of rice and vegetables, which form their staple food. They also eat fish and the flesh of any animal they can procure, except of the tiger, bear, and otter; and their time is mainly taken up with hunting, fishing, and agriculture. They moreover collect iron-ore, honey, and elephants' tusks, which they sell and barter for such luxuries as they cannot produce themselves. The principal occupations of their women are spinning, weaving, and cookery, besides which they also assist the men in their field labours. What they are, however, most remarkable for is the custom of tattooing their faces, which makes them hideous, though the marks and figures drawn are in themselves often very artistic and curious. The origin of the practice is thus accounted for:—They say that the Tártárs in the days of their power imposed upon all their subject races the payment of a tribute in women, whereupon the Khyen ladies decided on sacrificing their charms so as to make the tribute from their tribe unacceptable. The plan must have been eminently successful; it is certain that the custom of tattooing is now on the decline. The dress of the women consists of a black petticoat reaching to the knee, with a looser garment over it, while that of the men comprises a piece of blue cloth wound round the loins with one end of it dangling before, and the other dangling behind, and a cloth wound round the head, a jacket being also worn by those who can afford to have one. The arms of the men are the spear, and crossbow and arrows; but they are used only against wild beasts, the Khyens having no other enemies to fight with. Their villages consist usually of from fifteen to twenty houses each, over which there is a headman called *Táyi* or *Nandáyi*. Each house has ordinarily two apartments only, one for sleeping and the other for cooking in; and underneath the floor are lodged their swine and poultry. On getting married the Khyen always goes to live with his wife at her father's house, and never brings her thence till after the birth of one or two children. No dowry is given at marriage, and the union is dissoluble at the will of the parties, at a moment's warning, without any reason being required to be assigned for the severance. There are feasts given on occasions of both marriages and deaths, the choicest delicacies indulged in being pork and rice-beer. The religion of the race is confined to the propitiation of spirits, to whom sacrifices are made. The dead are burnt, and their bones buried in some distant mountain.

PART III.

GENERAL REMARKS.

THE stages of wild life are the savage and hunter state, the nomadic or herdsman state, and the agricultural state; of which the first appears to have long been passed by most of the tribes to whom we have referred, for, though hunting be still an occupation well prized by many of them, there is not one that lives by it exclusively at this day. Even the second stage has been passed by several tribes, though by far the greater number of them have only partially abandoned it, living as nomadic-cultivators, which is a compound of the second and third stages, and in different grades of advancement in that state. Under a well-ordered Government, the nomadic state is of course being rapidly changed for the agricultural one; but up to this time there are more nomadic cultivators among the wild tribes than regular tillers of the soil. The mode of cultivation followed is, we have seen, exceedingly simple and primitive, and almost identical in all places, though the races practising it are widely separated from, and have almost no sort of connexion with, each other. It has different names in different places, being called *dhái-yá* in the Central Provinces, *jooming* in the Hill Tracts of Chittagong, *toung-yá* in Arracan, etc.; but the process followed, which we have described, is in every case the same. All the tribes are given to living on the skirts of forests, mainly for the facility it gives them to effect clearances in the manner to which they are so partial. Few of them cultivate the same field more than two or three years, by which time the soil is held to have become perfectly exhausted, when they move on to new unbroken forests, never thinking of returning to the old ones till they have relapsed to their original jungly state. As there is abundance of virgin soil around them, they are thus constantly moving about by choice; and the herdsman's life which they also follow offers no hindrance to this, since they always carry their flocks and herds with them, it being, in fact, imperative on them to do so, owing to the general scantiness of the food-grains raised by them. The wildernesses roamed through also abound with game of all kinds, such as the bison, the buffalo, the elk, the wild hog, and the hare, and these form additional food articles for them, which makes them almost independent of their crops in unfavourable seasons. The jungles abound, moreover, with tigers, hyænas, and wolves; and it is a matter of necessity to the tribes living with them to acquire the art of killing them, and hence the prolonged indulgence of the hunting propensity in them even after the first stage of savage existence has been passed. It is this inclination of theirs, allied with their isolation, that seems to have taught them the more reprehensible use of their arms for which most of them were long so particularly famous. The roads from district to district necessarily passed over their hills and through their jungles, and this gave them the opportunity to levy tolls and blackmail from the traders and wayfarers who frequented them, which soon degenerated into open pillage and wholesale robbery, too often accompanied by the sacrifice of human lives.

Living in this manner, almost all the wild tribes have always remained confined within the nooks and corners into which they were forced when the immigrant races became a collected people, and have been necessarily far removed from the pale of civilisation. Of themselves, they have never sought, even in settled times, to cultivate the acquaintance of their neighbours, preferring to remain in barbarism in the hiding-places selected by their ancestors, and apparently thriving best in localities where no other human being could have existed. Those who live in forests say that they cannot endure the climate of the plains, where the heat gives them fever; those who inhabit the Terái, such as the Meches, have never attempted to get into higher ranges, which they assert do not agree with them; and those living inland, such as the Gonds, find that the sea air is fatal to them. So unhealthy are the places they occupy, that even those people of the plains who are in the habit of periodically visiting them—such as elephant-hunters, corn-dealers, money-lenders, and the collectors of jungle produce—seldom return from their annual expeditions without suffering in health, and yet none of the wild tribes betray any trace of sickliness about them, exhibiting, on the contrary, the most wonderful immunity from the effects of the malaria in which they live imbedded. This may, perhaps, be accepted as a proof of the antiquity of the races concerned, for they must have occupied their present corners for many centuries to have become so well acclimatised to them. The jungles are thinly populated, and, as a rule, the wild tribes procreate scantily, which accounts for their not being seen to increase in numbers in any place; and in particular localities they have further done all in their power to limit population by the adoption of such institutions as polyandry and infanticide. But they are hale and hearty-looking everywhere, much more so, certainly, than the natives of the plains, who are increasing in numbers at a rate that threatens to be perplexing to the politicians and administrators of a future day; and the only explanation the result admits of is, that they have got quite accustomed to live and thrive on the noxious exhalations they inhale.

The oldest Hindu books, again, speak of the *Dasyas* as a black race, and most of the internal tribes we have described are found to be very much darker than the Hindus and Mahomedans by whom they are surrounded, which may be accepted as another proof of their antiquity, since they must have occupied their present habitations in their distinctness from time anterior to or coeval with the establishment of the Hindu and Mahomedan races around them, and refused ever after to intermix with them. They have lived almost wholly by themselves, and where they have done so have retained their original colour undiluted, and not their colour only, but all the other peculiarities by which they were distinguished from the commencement. Almost all these races have less height, less symmetry, and more dumpiness and flesh than the peoples surrounding them; broader and flatter faces, shorter and wider noses, smaller eyes, larger ears, thicker lips, and deficient beards. In their eagerness to be considered respectable they often pretend to a descent from the Rájpoots; but the proofs patent in their features are unmistakable, and proclaim them to be of much older date than the Rájpoots, or their ancestors the Kshetriyas, can count in India. In the case of the frontier tribes their resemblance in features to the races living beyond them is easily traced; all the tribes on the western frontier having the Afghán or Beloochee appearance stamped on them; all those on the northern frontier bearing as deeply indented marks of a Thibetan origin; all those on the eastern frontier, of Burmese extraction; and all those on the north-eastern frontier exhibiting a compound of the Burman and Chinese features blended in varied shades. This proves the tribes to be either half-breeds or immigrants of old date long settled in the districts they now inhabit. But the features of the internal tribes are, like their colour, not traceable to any of the races surrounding them, and this distinctiveness they undoubtedly owe to the utter isolation in which they have always lived in their present quarters from the earliest times. Till recently they had no contact of any sort with aliens and strangers on any pretence whatever. The conveniences of life, where they had them, were such only as could be secured by self-labour, even the manufactures and arts being mostly domestic. Almost everywhere every man made his own house, conducted his own agriculture, and brewed his own beer, all which is done in most places in the same way even now. Smiths, carpenters, potters, and weavers did not exist before among them, and where existing at present are mostly foreigners recently admitted, and are barely allowed to live within hailing distance, not being suffered to intermix with them. It is not likely, therefore, that the dissimilarity so peculiar to the different tribes will be early effaced.

The blessings of civilisation among most of the tribes are now mainly represented by the presence of the *mahájuns*, money-lenders, and spirit-sellers, who have forced themselves into their company simultaneously with the artisan classes, in comparatively modern times. Their contact with these is generally held to have deteriorated their character; but this conclusion does not seem to be absolutely correct. If the intercourse has deteriorated their character to any extent in particular respects, it has certainly improved it in others in a greater degree; and their only hope of civilisation rests on such communion becoming closer day by day. What the Government has done amongst them is mainly confined to the putting down of the depredations and outrages which used to be so frequently committed by them, and this has been effected either by the strong hand of power, or by conciliation, or by compounding with their supposed rights to levy tolls or to pillage by paying regular stipends to them. Thus quieted, peaceful occupations have also commenced to be taught to them, which has induced habitual raiders and caterans to settle down as cultivators, and to colonise their own hill sides. But there was a mediatory go-between class wanted to humanise them, and, as none others cared to approach them, there was no option but to depend on the *mahájuns*, money-lenders, and spirit-sellers for exerting their kind offices in this way, to which they have done as much justice as could have been expected from them. The Gonds are said to have been at one time in the habit of feasting on their sick relatives, and even now some small tribes in Amarkantak and Chatisgurh have the credit of doing so. If these practices have declined in the greater part of their country at the present day, as they have undoubtedly done, that is solely attributable to the good offices of such intervening classes as the Brinjáris.

Nothing tends so much to confusion as excessive generalisations, and the good faith and manly character evidently belonging to some tribes have been very wrongly understood to be common to many of them. The truthfulness and honesty of some of the races are certainly remarkable, at least in their dealings with each other. Their right to the soil appropriated by them they consider to be unquestionable. "I am the proprietor of the land" is the boast alike of the Bheel, the Gond, the Meená, and the Sonthál. But this is only an assertion of right as against the Sovereign and the zemindár; no conflict arises among themselves on this account. When one person has commenced operations on a particular spot, no other man ever comes forward to claim it. When crops are raised they are cut and gathered without any contention. In several places even the granaries are left unprotected and unsecured, as no one ever thinks of appropriating what does not belong to himself. And the flocks and herds of different owners constantly run into each other without causing much quarrel or ill-feeling between them. These, however, are the usual Arcadian traits of savage life all over the world, and the same man who will not harbour a thought of over-reaching or robbing his brother savage unhesitatingly waylays, robs, and even murders without compunction the unwary traveller crossing his path. Here it is not so much an abstract question of honesty or dishonesty, as of the form in which they are severally exhibited. The descriptions which represent the wild tribes as being simple-hearted, good-natured, and inoffensive, are true in their integrity only of such inland tribes as the Sonthâls, Koles, and Bhooyáns, and of such borderers as the Khásiáhs of Gurhwál and Kumáon, but not of the rest. Many of the tribes have been lauded, and justly, for their love of truth and high-mindedness; but these are common traits with men who have always lived free. A rude respect for women has also been counted as the distinguishing virtue of some tribes; but that respect seems often to be qualified in several places to a considerable extent. The Khonds admit women into their general councils, but bring forward no subjects before them which have not been previously sat upon. The Meekirs eat tiger's flesh, but withhold it from their females lest it should make them too strong-minded for control. The Boksás do not allow their women to drink spirits, on the plea that their condition and duties do not require the use of stimulants. Among most of the tribes, moreover, the hardest drudgeries of life are always imposed on the women, and the show of respect towards them virtually resolves itself only to a concession made for reconciling them to their lot. A few tribes excepted, almost all the others have always had the credit of great agility and bravery, which combined to make them the good caterans in their native fastnesses which till recently they were. This pluckiness is, in the eyes of Englishmen, their highest virtue, and advantage has already been taken to convert those into soldiers whom it was possible to trust with arms and accoutrements. There are Bheel, Mair, and Kookie corps in the Indian service at this moment; the Bhaugulpore Hill Rangers, when they existed, were composed of Páháriáhs; and the police battalions all over the country include a large number of local wild men in their ranks. But with this pluckiness were allied a multitude of sins which it was not possible for it either to cover or palliate. All these spirited tribes are likewise spoken of as being hospitable, and some of them as being even social. But their hospitality and sociality have invariably been represented by a continued round of festivities and debaucheries, from one end of the year to the other, which has contributed more perhaps than anything else to their degradation. That examples so bright might never be lost sight of, it is the practice, we have seen, with some tribes to hang up the skulls of the animals killed and eaten in the halls of the entertainers, as records of their worth and for inciting their children to follow in their footsteps. After this, it is scarcely right to attribute any degeneracy in their character to their dealings with the *mahájuns* and money-lenders, or even to their connexion with the spirit-sellers. Of course the spirit-seller does a great deal of mischief wherever he goes; but the appetite he goes to feed existed in all the wilds and mountain fastnesses of India long before he approached them. Among several races we see private morals so carefully watched over that the unmarried youths of both sexes are kept apart at night, not only from each other, but even from the married members of their own families, lest there should be any lapse of virtue within the family circle itself; but we read in the same breath of such beastly customs as the *Bandana* among the Sonthâls, and the promiscuous intercourse of the sexes in various other shapes among many of the other tribes; of the wide prevalence of polygamy and polyandry; and of marriages taking place on credit, and the free exchange and divorce of wives. Among the Bheels, Mairs, Khonds, and others, a man takes a wife and keeps her so long as he likes her, but when they get tired of each other he transfers her, or she transfers herself, over to a third person without hesitation; and among the Kookies all the women of a village, married or unmarried, are at all times available to the chief at his will. In communities where such practices have long been in existence, even the spirit-seller had hardly any greater enormity to introduce.

Few of the wild tribes have any religion of their own, or any adequate idea of God, though they all, more or less, admit His existence, and even the existence of the soul and of futurity. All their notions on these subjects are, in fact, seemingly borrowed from among the superstitions of their neighbours; and in this way Hinduism has been acting with much force on them, and is fast drawing them down into its own vortex, which may in the future give them a civilisation such as it is not in the power of the Government to confer. Most of the divinities set up at present are the ogres of Hindu mythology, and the worship everywhere, except among the Himálayan tribes, is devil-worship *par excellence*, which was always attended in the past—that is, so long as it was possible for it to be so attended—with human sacrifices. But this state of things must mend when the adoption of Hinduism is complete and its better features are appreciated. The rites which have been most widely accepted up to this time are those observed on occasions of births, marriages, and deaths, all of which are followed with much fidelity; and there is certainly nothing particularly revolting in them. As a rule the wild tribes are even more superstitious than the Hindus; but they have this advantage over them, that they are not priest-ridden to the same or to any great extent. The Bráhman was an object of hatred to all of them, and they allow no interference on the part of their priest (the substitute of the Bráhman among them) with their domestic duties and affairs. Where any interference in such matters is called for, it comes from the elders of the people chosen by themselves, or from their chiefs, the priest's duties being confined to the celebration of the festivals; and this is an enormous advantage, the effects of which ought to be very salutary.

General Briggs, in his *Lecture on the Wild Tribes*, sums up the differences between them and the Hindus to the following effect:—(1) The Hindus are divided into castes; the aborigines have no such distinctions: (2) The Hindu widows do not remarry; the widows of the aborigines do, mostly taking the younger brothers of their former husbands: (3) The Hindus venerate the cow and abstain from beef; the aborigines feed on all flesh alike: (4) The Hindus abstain from drinks; the aborigines delight in them, and even their religious ceremonies are not complete without them: (5) The Hindus prepare their own food, or take only what has been prepared by a higher caste; the aborigines partake of food prepared by any one: (6) The Hindus do not shed blood habitually; but no ceremony of the aborigines is complete without the shedding of blood: (7) The Hindus have a caste of priests; the aborigines select their priests out of those particularly skilled in magic, or sorcery, or divination, or in curing diseases, etc.: (8) The Hindus burn their dead; the aborigines mostly bury them: (9) The Hindu civil institutions are municipal; those of the aborigines are patriarchal: (10) And, lastly, the Hindus have known letters and sciences and the art of writing for more than three thousand years; while the aborigines are, now at least, illiterate. This comparison does not show that the aborigines were in many respects open to further deterioration of character by coming into contact with the Hindus. The Hindus are a cleanly people, while the aborigines are excessively dirty, and are now only barely learning the use of water from their neighbours. Some of the frontier tribes, who are not aborigines, are certainly better housed, better fed, and better clothed than those of the plains; but this, which reads as an anomaly, is easily accounted for. Their food is more easily got, and, as they have no prejudices of caste, they do not stick at anything, several tribes not objecting to feed even on tigers, rhinoceroses, dogs, and vermin of all kinds, which always gives them variety and abundance, if not provisions of the choicest kinds. Their clothing is more difficult to get at; but, being absolutely necessary, owing to the climate of their hills and forests, has to be got, and is got, mostly from the civilised races living beyond their limits. Their houses, for the same reason, have to be better and more strongly built, and, the materials for them being easily available in their forests, it was not difficult to learn the art of so constructing them. These advantages apart, they have none over the people of the plains; and, if they are ever humanised to any appreciable extent, it must be by imitating them.

INDEX.

THE END.

THOS. DE LA RUE AND CO., PRINTERS, BUNHILL ROW, LONDON.